Loving Me

Loving Me

After Abuse

Angela Williams

BOOKLOGIX®

Alpharetta, Georgia

ISBN: 978-1-6653-0665-2 - Paperback
eISBN: 978-1-6653-0666-9 - ePub

Library of Congress Control Number: 2023912704

☉This paper meets the requirements of ANSI/NISO Z39.48-1992 (Permanence of Paper)

Cover Design: Shan Wallace, SDW Design :: Atlanta, GA :: 678-446-1273 shan@gamads.com

071323

I dedicate *Loving Me: After Abuse* to one of my dearest friends Polly Moore. Polly passed away on September 15, 2022. She suffered horrendous abuse from age eight to twelve and was tormented with pain and residual trauma of abuse late into her forties. She found healing through an organization I founded in 2007, VOICE Today, that provided hope and healing to survivors of child sexual abuse.

Her life, after her healing discovery, was lived to the fullest, emotionally, but in her midlife she was diagnosed with an autoimmune disease that attacked her liver and deteriorated her health. She often said the suffering lasted too long and her physical body paid the price. She was taken much too soon, the day after her sixtieth birthday.

I dedicate this book to Polly, as well as all survivors of abuse—those I know Polly would want to find healing as early in life as possible, so their pain doesn't become so toxic as to impact health and lifespan.

I write this book in honor of Polly, who wanted nothing more than for her family, friends, known and unknown, to live happily, whole, and with hope to the fullest, emotionally and physically. I miss her every day. So, Polly, I pray this book makes you smile!

TABLE OF CONTENTS

FOREWORD

This foreword is written to the love of my life, Angela. My meager words captured here will never begin to express the depth of our connection or the amazing life journey that God blessed me with when He intersected our paths. There is a Rascal Flatts song, "Bless the Broken Road," that speaks so profoundly to our ordained destiny. Well, God took the broken roads of our two lives and I know He led us to each other, as there is no other earthly explanation for where we both have come from to be where we are today.

The first time I saw Angela, all I could think about was how amazingly beautiful she was with her long dark hair, big brown eyes, perfect smile, and a glow that captivated me. When I was introduced to her, there was an inner strength I could sense, but there was something else that seemed to trigger an intrigue about her.

As our relationship grew, I could sense this joy, strength of character, a determination about her that I don't think she was even aware of, but I could also sense a depth of pain and sorrow lying underneath. The best way for me to describe it is with the analogy of an iceberg. I was seeing the 10 percent that was above the surface but this other 90 percent unknown part of her was underneath the surface. Over time, this 90 percent consisting of the pain, sorrow, grief, shame, fear, depravity, anger, resentment, and unworthiness that came from fourteen years of sexual abuse, abandonment, and neglect surfaced. It has been a mountain that we have had to climb and struggle with during our thirty-seven years of marriage while raising two children. Growing up with this kind of trauma as part of Angela's childhood, the concern and level of awareness that we protected them, and the ministry work that we were all a part of, was not easy on our family.

Our marriage survived the rigors of the mountain and is now rock solid. Our two children are grown and pursuing lives that are rewarding, fulfilling, and serving others.

My family had its own share of dysfunction, and as a child I prayed every day for a "Happy Family." It didn't happen during my childhood, so I made the commitment that when I married, it was going to be for better or for worse, for richer or for poorer, till God called one or both of us home. Divorce was not going to be an option. In the eighteen months of our dating relationship, Angela revealed to me some (not all) of her abuse history, but enough for me to get a picture of what she had suffered, and her vulnerability drew me even closer to her. I fell in love with Angela, all 100 percent of her, and I know God knit us together.

I made the mistake the first three or four years of our marriage of trying to "fix" her brokenness. When she would wake up in a night-terror, crying in her sleep from the nightmares, I would give her advice or relay that she was safe, say that it would never happen again, or some lame statement about getting past it. My "fix-it" words were not what she needed to hear. It took me a couple of years, and some very good advice, but I finally learned that what she needed to hear from me was "I love you," "I will never leave you or abandon you," "I am so sorry you suffered," "I will walk with you through this," "We will get through this." I finally realized that I needed to be compassionate, present, and patient.

I encourage anyone who is reading this book to read her first book, *From Sorrows to Sapphires,* which describes what she endured and journals how she was able to break the chains of being a victim, to moving past being a survivor, to finally having victory and reclaiming who she was meant to be.

God called her to write her first book and once it was written, He used her to start ministering and counseling others who had suffered abuse. That inner strength and determination I saw in her when we first met, empowered and motivated by the Holy Spirit, ignited a passion in her for advocacy. Over a ten-year period, and on a shoestring budget through Angela's organization, she and her team ministered to thousands of men, women, and children. Each person who shared their experience and their struggles connected to Angela and she to them. They could sense that she had gone through similar, if not identical, suffering and struggles. Each time she would counsel someone, it was like she took some of this pain, shame, and resentment on herself. I could sense it and started to prepare myself for the next days and sometimes weeks it took for her to process through the pain.

I started praying that God would keep this from happening, that He would allow her to be able to connect and have the same healing and encouraging words that would help, without her taking on this pain herself. On a men's weekend retreat, I was praying for this again during my quiet time and I felt God speak to me. That gut revelation that is profound and so much deeper than anything I would ever understand, could only come from the Holy Spirit. What I heard was Him explaining to me that He was turning a mess into a message. What was meant for evil and bad, He would turn into something meant to restore and make good. He revealed that Angela is able to connect to people and to their source of pain and suffering because of what she had endured and had overcome. The apostle Paul had prayed for a thorn to be removed from his side and God did not remove it. I don't know what Paul's thorn was or why God chose not to remove it. However, in that quiet time, I discerned that what I was praying for God to remove from Angela was her thorn in the side. I had a revelation that her connecting and carrying some of this pain from others was, in fact, a power source, a connection point for her ability to help heal those broken places in people's lives. I started crying—bawling, in fact. For one, I was not going to get what I was praying for, but two, I understood what God was saying and felt a little ashamed for asking for something selfish.

I learned on that weekend that we cannot live out a genuine Christian walk trying to fit God into our worldly story, but we need to gain a new perspective of realizing how we fit into God's eternal story.

Angela can only do what she does with God's grace, mercy, power, and strength. Thank goodness His mercies are new every morning. The purpose for our lives is to love God with all our hearts, all our minds, and all our strength, and to love our neighbors as ourselves. How can we love our neighbor as ourselves if we don't first love ourselves? How can we love ourselves without first understanding how much God loves us and the original plans and purposes He had ordained for us?

The iceberg analogy has totally shifted. That 90-percent portion that was under the surface, consisting of pain, sorrow, grief, shame, fear, depravity, anger, resentment, and unworthiness, is no longer the unseen mass dictating her direction pushed by the currents of life.

I pray that this book, *Loving Me: After Abuse*, is as impactful and inspirational as I know the truth, honesty, and radical life change that Angela has experienced. That thorn is still there, as I know how much love Angela has for God, for herself, and for all the hurting people who have suffered from abuse. Without this love, I know she would not be able to do what God has called her to.

What is God calling you to? I know He has plans and purpose for your life, and I hope this book and the other resources available through Angela's Voice will help you to heal and start to love yourself the way God loves you.

— Phillip Anthony Williams

CHAPTER 1

Loving Me

"Come to me, all you who are weary and burdened, and I will give you rest. Take my yoke upon you and learn from me, for I am gentle and humble in heart, and you will find rest for your souls. For my yoke is easy and my burden is light" (Matthew 18:28-30).

After abuse . . .

I really only have one memory before my abuse: I was playing in a wooden crib and vaguely remember my favorite uncle picking me up and doting on me. He was nicknamed "Uncle

Puff" because he smoked. I remember giggling and feeling happy in that memory, feeling light. I then remember being so very sad in the next. The dark had come. The heaviness of fear dictated my thoughts.

I have struggled my entire life to restore that innocent carefree child and to love myself. To love who I was meant to be before abuse.

From that moment on, all I can remember was being brutally berated, beaten, and abused. The first memory of this abuse, I was almost three years old. The abuse lasted until age seventeen, at which time I was in a deep dark hole. The abuse was multilayered, multifaceted. I suffered vile verbal abuse that included constant cursing, demeaning slurs, and painful physical abuse— slaps, punches, kicks, and striking with belts, shovels, and anything handy my stepfather could grab. The sexual abuse for a little body was unbearable. I'll spare the details as I know it is hard to fathom that an adult man would slaughter the innocence of a three-year-old child. I feel sorry for her and even more sorry for someone who possesses that much evil.

My biological father left my mother and me at birth. That, too, left a profound wound of abandonment in my heart. When I was only days old, he walked away, washed his hands of me, and never looked back. He, too, lives with his own giant, one that, it seems, he has never been able to overcome. A short time after they were married, my mother discovered he had epilepsy. It impacted his ability to function, to be a stable provider and marriage partner. The disease apparently altered his personality and spun him into a tunnel of depression where he resides, distant from me and from my love. I keep waiting and hoping for a phone call, a card, or a visit, but it never comes. As an eternal optimist, I look for those acts, but the reasonable dream of a little girl for an engaged, loving daddy remains unfulfilled. It is hard to hold on to hope, so I surrender and say, "Please, God, if it be in your will. Please, God, I want him to know my love and welcome my love."

After a brief meeting in a laundromat and a two-week courtship, my mother married a man I was immediately forced to call "Daddy" from the age of three. In hindsight, it seemed to me that my mother was desperate for a partner and a father for me. She told me that memories of her childhood are blighted by events she can't remember, pain she dares not recall. She said she never felt wanted or loved and that somewhere in her childhood, this limiting belief stole her confidence.

My stepfather, full of evil, observed a fragile single mom that he could control (and subsequently control me) without much resistance. My mother, refusing to face a second failed marriage, succumbed to his iron hand of abuse, and her attempts to protect me were futile, and she ignored the silent tsunami of sexual abuse. She was trapped in the crosshairs of domestic violence, without the power or will to escape. I think it was just too awful for her to face, so she turned a blind eye.

It was an era of silence. It was a time of closed doors, and no one dare to peak in. Unfortunately, those doors are still closed today for many children abused behind those doors. Many—too many—in my life turned a blind eye to what they knew was happening behind our closed doors. In the '60s and '70s, you minded your own business and looked the other way. My extended family did the same—they looked the other way. Abuse is very messy, and if outsiders get involved, they may step into the minefield themselves, making it easier to ignore so their life doesn't get messy. I challenge the thought that those complacent are also culpable. I encourage everyone to *not* be complacent and always stand up for victims, especially if they have an intuition that a child is being abused. You are their only voice. I had no voice and no one with the courage to intervene, regardless of the obvious signs that I was being abused. No one cared enough to get their hands messy.

That word "abuse" has so many dimensions, and those who have been abused have a difficult time defining all that happens during the horrific experience. The pain cuts deep, introduces chronic fear, and impacts so many aspects of our lives, not the least our value and self-worth. It's challenging to put into words because abusers manipulate our emotions with every attack, and every attack hurts more severely than the last. With each attack, you become weaker, more fearful, and more defeated. It's as if the abuse whittles away a part of you.

I tried to create a thick skin of survival to deflect the pain but the scarred layers just seemed to absorb every word and every strike. Abuse made me numb. Stuffing down the painful emotions served me well until the day I wanted to feel. When you want to feel yet you can only feel numb, it's frightening. I am a person with a lot of love to give, but with numb emotions, it's a recovery of connection. I had to try hard multiple times to love intentionally despite how hurt I was.

Child victims are defenseless. It is impossible to defend yourself against a psychopath whose single goal is to destroy a life. Murder can happen in an instant or in methodical, planned routine attacks. Regardless, if not murder of the body, it is murder of a soul and, ultimately, all within.

We struggle to comprehend the depths of the trauma, and there is still so much to learn about the aftermath. We fight to block abuse memories — I've described it as trying to hold a beach ball under water 24/7, an exhausting task. I had an inner narrative that seared into my thoughts. I blamed myself, my abuser so masterful in his attacks that he made me feel as though I deserved the abuse. Because the abuse was so horrible and unbearable, I began to take on the identity that I was horrible and unbearable, making me feel unlovable. I was caught in a web of lies that entrapped me.

The abuse is akin to man o' war jellyfish, with tentacles that wrapped around our mind, body, and soul so tight we can't breathe. The tentacles' painful stings paralyze our body, and we don't have the strength to tear out of this slimy web, let alone defend ourselves. Like the sting, the pain lingers, but unlike the sting of a man o' war, this sting can linger for years. The abuse overwhelms our strength, our mind, our body, and our soul.

I've tried to minimize and marginalize what was the most horrific emotional and physical violence a human can endure. I believe that family members who witnessed some of the abuse also want to minimize and marginalize for their own sanity. I encourage everyone not to fall into the trap as I did where I tried to believe their narrative versus the truth. They say things like, "Did that really happen?" "Are you making more out of this?" or "Are you blowing this out of proportion?" Well, let me say unequivocally— YES, it really happened, and it was that brutal and that horrific.

There were many days I prayed to die so I didn't have to face the next day, the next rape, the next round of strikes, the next verbal berating by my stepfather. The piercing pain of being abandoned by my father and neglected by my mother made me feel lost. From the tender age of three to age seventeen, the daily cruelty and defilement I endured ravaged my childhood, my value, my self-respect and my self-confidence. I learned to loathe myself in light of these sad circumstances.

Abuse is abuse. No matter what someone has endured, it changes them forever, and not always for the worse. We must change the narrative. The abuse did not *destroy* me, it made me *stronger*. I find I have an unmatched resilience, compassion, and appreciation for peace. I try to never take a day of peace for granted. It takes a conscious effort to heal from such severe trauma. The world says, "Get over it." I say let's heal and OVERCOME IT so as to not rob anyone of one more day of harmony. Our mental health is just as important as our physical health, and if you have been abused, I pray everyone take the steps to heal, to grieve, and to recover. Abuse has robbed many days of joy in my life and from those closest to me.

No more, because I am important—my healing is important to my health, my life, and those who love me.

I've learned that a critical step on this healing journey is to learn to love myself in light of horrific circumstances that taught me to hate myself. I've spent the last forty-plus years working on restoring and healing with great progress and now, diving into what I feel is the last frontier—learning to love myself after the abuse. I transparently share this journey because it is my hope and desperate prayer that my words can bring suffering to an end for everyone who has endured abuse and help them say enough is enough.

It's time to heal. It's time to turn the chaos into peace, to calm the storms in our life so the sun can brightly shine. I am ready and willing to reclaim my power, my self-respect, my value, my healing, and ultimately my life. I want to love myself unconditionally and completely. Not in a narcissistic, selfish way, but in a compassionate, sympathetic process. I cried for years and slept on a tear-soaked pillow in pain. The night I was able to sleep on a dry pillow was a good night. The next day was an epiphany that I had turned a corner. I had made progress. I could really heal from this mess. Wow! It was a good day.

Public journeys are never pleasant—you become vulnerable to the world. As my pastor Craig Mosgrove said, "Writing bares your mind, body, spirit, and soul." I have to be vulnerable and tell you that I have struggled with this book, second-guessing and lamenting over what should be written. I want to disclose that this book is solely written from my heart to those who have been abused. You will not find perfection or a quick-step guide to healing, but what I do hope you find is an honest account of my journey to figuring out how to love myself after abuse.

Fortunately, I have some experience. I bared my soul in my first book, my memoir, *From Sorrows to Sapphires,* so I have some experience with bleeding on pages. It was a difficult process but rewarding. By sharing my story, I continue to receive more healing and am inspired by the lives it has touched. I am committed to sharing everything I feel meaningful to help everyone's journey to healing. I once heard there is so much more room on the outside than on the inside, so I encourage everyone, if you don't already, to journal your feelings. When you open up your wounds through writing, you find some who will cheer and some who will be critical. That's okay. At my age, I know all too well that God is my judge and my jury.

I am lucky to have found an intimate relationship with Jesus as well as the path to healing in my thirties and have traveled it since. Sadly, many don't find this path. They suffer in silence. Without healing intervention, it is common for a child who has suffered from abuse to be subjected to abuse their entire life by multiple abusers, unable to break the cycle. Domestic and child abuse is most often a silent epidemic, happening behind closed doors and never reported to law enforcement. As a result, the suffering continues in silence and justice is denied.

I have worked with thousands of victims of abuse, both physical and sexual, for decades, and the common theme is that they struggle with a spirit of self-hatred and self-destruction, which plagues their lives. This often plays out in addiction to sex, drugs, and alcohol, which aids in numbing the pain of abuse but destroys lives. My journey was riddled with both self-hatred and self-destructive thoughts and behaviors. I've had little mercy for myself. Sadly, I rarely gave myself grace for faults or failures. I rarely had confidence in my decisions. I wanted to please everyone, I wanted to be liked, loved, adored by all. That is rare in real life.

I think we expect a straight vertical trajectory of healing, but it looks more like a stock market graph. Up, down, sideways. Life gives us deep dips, hyper-highs, and lingering lows. Before I realized I needed to make a conscious effort to heal and seek professional help, I was screaming inside, suffering in silence, finding it almost impossible to even take a deep cleansing breath. I suffered debilitating flashbacks, nightmares, and cried many nights into my pillow, for fear that speaking the dark secret would cause me to be totally ostracized from society.

That silence kept me sick, both mentally and

physically. I learned to believe lies over truth, either the ones society engraves in our minds or the unhealthy narrative I repeated to myself. Healing began when I said, "I NEED HELP!" I found the courage to share the darkest secrets and deep crevices of my pain. Telling my own story was a powerful way to take back my life, and professional counseling was a critical part of my healing. The worldly view of professional counseling is seen a sign of weakness. Well, I disagree. Asking for help in desperate times is no sign of weakness.

There is help all around, but in times of distress, we often can't see the forest for the trees. I have found help in many places: help from above, in conjunction with professional help, help from friends and family. I learned to silence the noise of the world and welcomed help. I had to lay my pride down because pride often got in my way — pride of not wanting to be vulnerable, pride of not wanting to share my past, my pain, my ugliness. I also began to be still and listen to God.

> *"Come to me, all you who are weary and burdened, and I will give you rest. Take my yoke upon you and learn from me, for I am gentle and humble in heart, and you will*

find rest for your souls. For my yoke is easy and my burden is light" (Matthew 18:28–30).

I desperately wanted rest for my soul. I felt as though I had been fighting my whole life, a war raging inside to find peace and quiet. The war of my childhood had wreaked so much havoc on the opportunity for tranquility. It was in those dark valleys, seeking peace and truth, that I truly drew closer to God. Healing began in the quiet surrender, moment by moment, day by day, year by year. I wish I could say it was an instant, but it wasn't. It was repeatedly choosing health, laying down my pain, and asking God to redeem it and heal it, to use it to make my sisters' and brothers' journey easier. That may not make much sense, but I wanted the instant mix, and I got the crock-pot version. Patience is not my strong suit.

I know in the crevices of my soul that God has been working on me to truly love myself. The self-love I am speaking of is not a selfish love but a genuine, selfless love full of self-respect and acceptance — loving the person God created me to be absent of the ugly abuse I suffered, loving *me*, honestly, "the good, the bad and the ugly."

Let's face it, we all have the "good, the bad, and the ugly." I hear the soundtrack theme in my mind to the Clint Eastwood movie, *The Good, the Bad and the Ugly*. It's a classic and a favorite movie in my family. As a survivor of abuse, it's difficult to be vulnerable and expose my struggles, my weaknesses, and even — sad to say — my strengths. I am learning to be authentic and genuine in every aspect of my life, and thus, that requires vulnerability. This is the love I desperately want for myself and to share with others: I want to love myself enough to be truly transparent. I am not perfect, and I don't have all the answers, but what I have learned I want to share to help make everyone's journey easier.

The mountain I continue to march around is truly learning how to love myself in this way, accepting that God created me and loves me unconditionally. There is nothing I can do to make God love me more, and nothing I can do to make God love me less — even if *I* have loved *me* less. God still loves me and is with me. In God's word, He tells us:

> *"For the entire law is fulfilled in keeping this one command: "Love your neighbor as yourself" (Galatians 5:14).*

I hear God say, "It's all right Angela, I know you have not always known pure and true love. You have suffered, and you have great fear, but it's all right, I am here. I am here and I love you." God loves us with a pure love, and He truly intended for us to love ourselves. When the Pharisee asked Jesus, "What must I do to inherit eternal life? He answered:

> *"'Love the Lord your God with all your heart and with all your soul and with all your strength and with all your mind'; and, 'Love your neighbor as yourself."*
>
> *"Jesus continued, 'You have answered correctly,' Jesus replied. 'Do this and you will live'"* (Luke 10:27-28).

It is my desire that I live, and my prayer is that you live, the life God intended. Not a life of torment, but a life of abundant peace and joy. The mountain is steep and the struggle is real, but through these pages I pray I can inspire you to love yourself as God loves you and truly walk in your identity in Christ Jesus.

It took me a long time, but I pray this book can be a shortcut for you to receive the pure, all-encompassing, eternal love of God. I pray my words touch your heart and help you draw closer to the true source of healing.

Healing is a journey that starts by taking that first step. Let us climb this mountain together, and when we arrive at the peak, we can rejoice in the complete healing that God desires for each of us. We will overcome the evil perpetrated against us; we will learn, though painfully, to understand that our abusers are influenced by evil forces, but they, too, deserve forgiveness and the hope of salvation.

I invite you to begin the vertical climb with me. Don't look down—look straight up. If you are in a hopeless place, may God give you the strength for renewed hope and may my words lead you to loving yourself more. Loving after abuse is the greatest gift we can give ourselves to heal. Loving yourself after abuse is the path to greater healing.

CHAPTER 2

Loving the Reflection

"The Lord your God in your midst, The Mighty One, will save; He will rejoice over you with gladness, He will quiet you with His love, He will rejoice over you with singing" (Zephaniah 3:17).

Some people look at me and see confidence and beauty, but I have seen a different reflection in the mirror. I have seen shame staring back at me. Who am I? When I look in the mirror, who do I see? Do I love the person looking back at me?

For many years, I could hardly look in the mirror. I was disgusted at the reflection of shame. I also made such bad choices that I thought God could never forgive. I was not raised in the church, so I did not understand "grace," the undeserved *favor* of God. That was foreign to me. I did not understand that the God who created me, loved me unconditionally, sent His Son to shed his blood in repentance for my sins, who took all my faults and failures and said, "It's okay, come to me. I forgive you." The sacrifice of Jesus built the bridge to God. It made me blemish-free in the eyes of God.

The shame separated me from God because I took on the blame for my abuse and thought God could not look at me with all this sin. Shame on me—literally. There was so much shame on me, I could not bear to look at myself because all I saw was the veil of perversion that covered me. As a young girl I would claw my face, trying to peel it off. I saw a weak person who could not protect herself.

Because of the perversion I had experienced, I felt distant from God, as if the evil perpetrated against me made me unfit to be a Christian, unfit to serve God. When I looked in the mirror, I was so ashamed—ashamed that I didn't have the voice to scream, ashamed that I didn't have the courage to make it stop, ashamed that my body even responded when my soul was screaming inside my mind, ashamed that I was compliant. But God kept knocking on my heart. God saw my mission; I saw pain. God saw my potential; I saw my obstacles. God saw my compassion; I saw my hardness. I saw someone that no one valued enough to protect. God saw someone worth rescuing. I saw the sick sexual acts I had been forced to endure—I was repulsed. God saw scars worth redeeming, and His blood on the cross covered that violation. I think God saw a girl, a mature woman, who would say, "Yes, God, I will stand in the gap." I saw the lies of my abuser who said I was worthless and deserved pain, including death. Yet I know I was always meant to live, but death has shadowed me. I have always felt the angels protecting me.

Through many years of God reaching for me, he finally pulled me out of the muck. He showed me miracles on a mission trip to Matamoros, Mexico, and the Spirit of the Lord came over me. I was ministering and praying as part of a medical mission team. I would pray for those who came for medical care in another room. The people would feel the anointing and have miraculous healing, visions, receive answers to prayers, and release strongholds in an instant.

Word spread that something incredible was

happening and people came for days, the line wrapping around the building, for their own personal experience with God. The unbelieving, the doubting, the desperate-for-answered-prayer came, and God used me to facilitate that life-changing encounter. When I tell you answered prayer manifested in our presence, it is the gospel truth. I have never experienced such an amazing, spirit-filled gifting like that before. Seeing and feeling the move of God will stay with me for the rest of my life. It was a glimpse of heaven. I was so overjoyed because the gap between my shame and God's glory was closing. Where I thought I could never be used by God, He showed me I could mightily be used by Him to help others heal.

I believe it happened because I had prepared myself in advance for the trip. I had prayed on hands and knees on a mat a friend had given me that said "PRAY AND SEEK" multiple times a day and devoted myself to this type of prayer, reading the Bible and fasting for three months prior to the mission trip. Through this dedicated time of prayer and fasting, I got my flesh out of the way and believed God for miracles.

> *"...if my people, who are called by my name, will humble themselves and pray*

and seek my face and turn from their
wicked ways, then I will hear from heaven,
and I will forgive their sin and will heal
their land" (2 Chronicles 7:14).

That mission trip was a spiritual marker in my journey of faith, as I witnessed firsthand the miracle making move of God. When you witness miracles, it moves your faith past complacency to a place of being totally sold out. When I woke in the morning to return home from the mission trip, after being in the presence of God, ministering for four days straight to the people of Matamoros, Mexico, and our fellow team, I felt the ominous *voice* of God—which if you have ever heard the voice of God, you cannot explain or deny it.

I felt, sensed, and heard God telling me not to get on the shuttle bus to the airport. I had a speaking engagement the following day, so I couldn't take the twenty-six-hour charter bus ride home; I was going to fly home with about ten of our mission trip members who also planned to fly. The other 120 or so of our group were going to take a coach bus back to Atlanta, including my husband, Phil, and our son.

I had the thickest, eeriest feeling. Ignoring the

voice of God, I got on the shuttle bus and headed to the airport in Brownsville, Texas, but still felt an impending gloom. It dawned on me that we would be crossing the US-Mexico border on the bus and I may be stopped. I had a previous issue with a mistaken identity once before returning from Italy. This had to be the cause for the eerie feeling I was experiencing, so I tried to alert and explain this to the team.

We got through the border crossing without incident, and still the bad feeling did not go away. Then, when I was on my way to the airline gate, it was as if I was walking through mud. God said, "Do not get on the plane." OMG—literally—I did not know what to do. My fellow team members already thought I was crazy because of the commotion and working of the Holy Spirit they had all witnessed.

So, I prayed. "God, these people think I am crazy, and You want me to tell them to not get on the only flight this afternoon back to Atlanta." I pleaded with God and the conversation went something like this:

> *"God, I know I hear You and sense that You are telling me not to get on this plane. Lord, can I walk in faith and ask You not*

*to put me in this position and ask You to
prevent any harm and protect this flight?"*

Oh, it was the boldest prayer of my life. I guess
since I had seen such miracles and had witnessed
healing and salvations, I was walking on Holy
water. I knew if I boarded the flight and it did go
down, I would die, but I would be with Jesus. So,
though I certainly wanted to live, I knew if I died,
it would be His plan.

We boarded the plane. I had always had a
crazy belief that if I were ever assigned the last
seat in the back row of a plane, it was going
down. Guess where my seat was? Yep, last
window seat on the left. I was freaking out. I got
my Bible out of my bag and began to pray. If there
was any doubt about my team members thinking
I was crazy before this, well, I took it up a notch.
I was in my window seat, praying in the Spirit,
reading scripture, pleading the blood of Jesus
over every person on that aircraft. The flight
started down the runway, it lifted up in the air,
and we were ascending.

The first hurdle had been crossed with takeoff,
and I breathed a sigh of relief — until I looked out
my window. I don't offer hyperbole to make it
any more than point of fact, but I feel I have to tell

you that I would swear on a stack of Bibles, while standing by my grandmother's grave, that what I saw is true: There was an angel, as big as the plane, outside my window.

What am I seeing? WHAT?

I was so shocked. She had a white satin robe and long shimmering blonde hair and I could not make out her face, only a bright glow. She stretched the length of the plane and what I focused on was that she had one hand on top of the wing and the other on the bottom of the wing.

At this exact moment, one of the doctors on our mission team screamed, "Oh my God!" I swung my head around toward him, and outside his window, I saw the faces of passengers on another plane. Still in shock from what I saw, I bluntly said without hesitation, "No worries, our angel is pulling our plane out of harm's way." It happened so fast, but he looked at me as if I had lost my ever-loving mind.

Well, it was reported a near miss of two planes over Brownsville, Texas, and we were one of those planes. To this day, the story doesn't even sound real, but I lived it and I know what I experienced. I know the power of God and the power of prayer. I walked through faith, but I would not recommend ever denying the Voice of

God and responding in disobedience. Pleading with God is a delicate undertaking, especially when you have heard clear instructions. This experience increased my faith, my confidence, and filled me with such joy. The reflection in the mirror was beginning to change.

I know God spared my life as He has many times. I treasure life and I lived through that experience, but as a young girl, I carried, like a badge, the spirit of death. I wanted to die, battled thoughts of suicide, and even gave in to them. These thoughts of death in my youth rolled around in my head constantly. Some of the vile slurs my stepfather spat at me are hard to forget: "If you were on fire, I would not spit on you," "You don't have the sense to get out of a shower of s**t," "Your own father didn't want you, he left you, so who would ever want you?" "You are so lazy; you don't deserve to be fed," "You'll never amount to anything, so don't try," and hundreds more hurtful words that pain me to recount them here. These were the curses he spoke over my life. These curses haunted me when I looked in the mirror.

The torture was relentless. He would lock me in his car in the middle of summer ninety-plus-degree heat until I gasped for air, while he shouted at me that I didn't deserve to breathe. Words that cut deep, curses that sealed insecurities, self-loathing, all to gain complete power and control of my mind, body, and spirit.

In my effort to heal I had to deliberately and intentionally rebuke and break the power of those curses on me. I'm sure if you are reading this, you may have had similar word-vomit spat upon you. When you are told by an abuser how very worthless you are, and when you are violated time after time with no way to defend yourself, it deteriorates your dignity. Dignity is defined as "the right of a person to be valued and respected for their own sake, and to be treated ethically." Ethics apply to morals—what is right or wrong—which in our world is deteriorating, being eroded and washed away at an alarming rate.

We should all be able to agree, though, that to attack a child verbally, physically, or sexually is wrong. Berating any human being, especially a child, by verbally abusing, beating, raping, and crossing personal boundaries should all be viewed as deplorable evil behavior.

Abuse is usually perpetrated behind closed doors. It's an act with few witnesses, and those who do witness often turn a blind eye. These attacks we endure torment us and strip us of our self-worth. Though our bodies may survive the attacks, our spirits are crushed. When my abuser stripped me of my value, self-respect, power, and voice, survival, and self-loathing were my primary thoughts. You don't know in those moments of abuse that the experience is life-altering. You don't know that ten, twenty, thirty, or forty-plus years later, you would still be dealing with the aftermath, because you look at the same face in the mirror every day.

Some people think you can just get over it. I understand you can't. It takes time, personal effort, a desire to heal, and the power of God working in your life. It takes help to rebuild what was destroyed. The abuse happens in isolation and society wants us to heal in isolation, because healing is often messy. Society's answer is to go behind doors an hour a week with a counselor and heal. Don't misunderstand, as I highly value therapy, but we need more than an hour a week to heal. We need a compassionate understanding tribe to help us heal. And we need Jesus.

In those horrific moments of abuse, death seemed more appealing. To be transparent, survival and hate were competing thoughts. I hated my abuser, truly hated him. I wanted him dead and thought of ways to kill him before the next attack. My coat of shame thickened, because how could a good person have such horrible thoughts?

Trauma causes distorted beliefs about ourselves and others; sometimes these beliefs are not true. One belief that I and many survivors I have worked with over the years have struggled with is that we are bad. It takes a lot of "reprogramming" to eliminate that lie and keep it from permeating into our rational thoughts. You see, if I think I am a bad person, and tell myself every day that I am a bad person, then I begin to believe I am a bad person. Even though that is certainly not rational, we base our every opinion upon that untruth. We may have even toyed with the thought, "The world would be better off without me." An absolute lie from the gates of hell. Those suicidal thoughts take root. Today, if I ever have a second where that thought creeps in, I immediately say out loud, "Satan, get behind me!" and I quote:

> *"Finally, brothers and sisters, whatever is true, whatever is noble, whatever is right, whatever is pure, whatever is lovely, whatever is admirable — if anything is*

> *excellent or praiseworthy — think about*
> *such things" (Philippians 4:8).*

Not only do abuse survivors feel bad on the inside but we also are critical of our bodies. The reflection in the mirror, to me, reflects a body I have never liked, to the point of being disgusted with the way I look. I, as many fellow survivors of abuse, have body image issues. I realize body image is a real struggle for many, but I believe it's even more so apparent for those who have been abused.

To be honest, I have never loved my body. I have been overweight for most of my adult life. Wow, that was hard to say, but it's the truth. In my fifties, I have probably tried every single diet plan out there, some more than once. I have success for some months, lose ten to twenty pounds, then fall off the wagon, and gain it all back, plus some. It's very defeating; I have conquered so much in my life, but my weight has been a lifelong struggle.

At seventeen, the last time I was abused, I weighed 125 pounds and was a perfect size six. I ran away from home at seventeen and began to stuff my mouth to help the pain. Within a year, I was 175 pounds and a size twelve. Turning to food as comfort, I doubled my size believing that would stop the wolf whistles and men's attention. I am well insulated and have since gained another forty-five pounds in subsequent years.

I struggled with bulimia in my teens and young adulthood. Gorging myself and then purging, the cycle was endless. It was a dark time in my life. I was a freshman in college, feeling lonely, with no family support, on my own. Money was short, so I worked as a waitress at the Moose Club, where fried seafood was plentiful. Thank God it was only a season, and I was able to stop purging. Extremes seem to have been a theme in my life.

I know how to lose weight: eating a low-calorie healthy diet and exercise. In my case, it really boils down to not prioritizing my health—before work, chores, and play. It's also an unhealthy combination of laziness and lack of self-control. Exercise is hard work, and I can always talk myself out of it as fast as I talk myself into it. I always feel so good after exercise and a healthy meal, but taking that step to get on the treadmill, on the exercise bike, or for that brisk walk is a constant battle, and I'm never consistent. I envy those people who are disciplined enough to exercise and stay fit. I can say, even though it is a battle, it is one I am committed to winning. I am giving myself grace in this area. I'm not giving up — if at first you don't succeed, try, try again.

I have begun to praise myself with a word of encouragement when I make good decisions and try not to beat myself up so hard for the bad ones. And, of course, there are those who have the opposite struggle — anorexia, refusing to eat, and obsessive exercise, struggling to maintain a healthy weight. I don't have experience with anorexia but if you want help with it or any eating disorder, I encourage you to seek professional counseling that specializes in eating disorders. I have also listed some online resources here:

- www.mannafund.org — Helps individuals who have life-threatening eating disorders to gain access to intensive treatment when they otherwise could not afford it.
- www.talkitout.org — Manna Fund has created a website to support those going through eating disorder recovery.
- www.nationaleatingdisorders.org — Nationally based organization regarding eating disorder information and connections.

- www.eatingdisorderhope.com —
  Vast amount of information on eating
  disorders.

Gisele Bundchen reports, "Since paring back her modeling commitments, she has dedicated herself to environmental activism, particularly with regard to the Amazon rainforest's conservation, and business ventures like eco-friendly skin care and a lingerie line. She has also been vocal about mental health, disclosing debilitating panic attacks that she said had her contemplate suicide and criticizing unrealistic beauty standards."[1] If the most beautiful, peak-paid model in the world has panic attacks related to body-image issues and suicidal thoughts, then throw out the window the belief that when we are a fit size six, we are going to be happy.

My cycle of self-criticism has been constant. I bear my soul to expose my vulnerability. So, I am determined to love the woman in the mirror, no matter the neon number on the scale. Don't get

---

[1] Leanne Italie and Fred Goodall, "Tom Brady, Gisele Bundchen divorce becomes official: 'we have grown apart,'" FOX 5 Atlanta, *Associate Press*, October 28, 2022, https://www.fox5atlanta.com/sports/tom-brady-gisele-bundchen-divorce-reports?utm_campaign=trueanthem&utm_medium=trueanthem&utm_source=facebook&fbclid=IwAR0J6mHpjse7fMJ7Ts1x6IF9d7BcrMTZTD8N-GGjEdV9K6-JuBz7kTe5vh0.

me wrong, I would love to arrive at my ideal weight. I truly want to be healthy into my winter season so I can enjoy all the days of my life.

It is a proven fact that eating less calories, making healthier food choices, exercising consistently, getting adequate sleep, and managing stress fosters good health. It's a constant battle, but I have changed my self-talk. Instead of being critical, I try to turn the narrative around to be encouraging. Choices are intentional decisions, with every decision being one step closer to our destiny. So, I try to make the choice that leads to health. When I fail, I extend grace and start again tomorrow.

I was recently diagnosed with a pleomorphic adenoma tumor in my parotid gland. The subsequent weeks of tests revealed the tumor was about two centimeters in diameter and benign. Surgery was scheduled to remove the tumor and my parotid gland on my left side. The surgery is somewhat involved because many of the facial nerves surround the parotid gland, which presents a risk of facial paralysis on my left side. I've had some pretty deep introspection and, I must admit, fear around the possibility of facial disfiguration.

I've contemplated how I would feel should the worst happen. Will I still love the woman in the mirror if she had a droopy eye and mouth? Would I still have the courage to stand in front of an audience and speak?

I asked the doctor, "Is surgery my only option?"

"Yes," she replied, "because the tumor is growing."

My daughter is a doctor and she said, "Mom, the tumor has to come out sooner than later."

Well life is always throwing us curve balls, so I wrestled with the risks of facial paralysis and concluded that it's better to be alive with possible side effects than six feet under with a tumor.

The answer is *yes*—I will still love the woman in the mirror, and these weeks of wrestling with this medical challenge has produced a resolve to face any challenges, knowing I have the strength from above and loving support of family and friends. Even deeper is coming to grips with the fact that whatever challenges lie ahead, it will not deter me from the work God has called me to achieve, which is helping others overcome abuse and protecting the next generation of children from abuse.

Another milestone on the journey to loving me is acknowledging truth.

Who am I? Sometimes our true self is right here, buried under the abuse, the curses, the cultural conditioning, other people's opinions, labels attached to us, and inaccurate conclusions we draw about ourselves that become branded in our belief system.

At my innermost being, I know I am a good person. I am a loving, kind, and generous person. I know my good qualities far outweigh the bad. I am a person who likes to win and cheer others' victories and wishes no harm to anyone but justice for all. I am a person who does not lie down and turn a blind eye to abuse. Never again will I allow myself to be abused, and I will advocate for others under the boulder of abuse.

This was the beginning of loving the person in the mirror. I now understand that just because horrible things happened to me, it does not make me a horrible person. Just because I made mistakes in an effort to survive and cope doesn't mean those mistakes define me. Just because I was exposed to darkness and perversion does not make me a dark and perverted person. This is my truth.

We must undo our thinking. For many years, I would write affirmations on my mirror so, when I looked at myself, these affirmations were a part of my reflection. These affirmations have become incantations in my spirit:

I love myself and I am loved.

I believe in myself.

I am a good person with good intentions.

I am enough. I have enough.

I am resilient. I can do hard things.
I am grateful for today and all it holds.

I am in the right place, at the right time, doing the right thing.

I accept myself just as I am without judgment.

I am safe and supported.

I trust I am healing even when I can't feel it.

I forgive because I am forgiven by Jesus.

You get the idea. You can make your own list, continue to add to this list, and relate them to your own struggles. I would write these in soap on my mirror and change them out with the messages I needed the most, at any given time in my healing journey. When negative thoughts creep in, as they often do, we have to be prepared with positive counter thoughts.

I am still human and healing; I can replace that thought with truth. What is your truth? Are there self-destructive thoughts that roll around in your head? What difference could it make if you were to counter these thoughts with powerful encouragement? I declare the promises of God over my life. These declarations are scriptures that debunk the lies of Satan; they are truths from God that I cling to daily:

Truth #1: God loves me unconditionally.

> *"For I am convinced that neither death nor life, neither angels nor demons, neither the present nor the future, nor any powers, neither height nor depth, nor anything else in all creation, will be able to separate us from the love of God that is in Jesus Christ our Lord" (Romans 8:38–39).*

Our world is sinful with many relationships that have strings attached and conditions to meet. Those closest to us sometimes disappoint us. We were born with a great need inside each of us to be loved forever, unconditionally, with an all-inspiring love that drives us to be a better human being and leave a legacy. God provides us with that love. Theologians have said, "We have a God-shaped hole in our heart; that space only God can fill." And the love we need is strong, unshakable, and everlasting, given by our Creator to share with others. This love I am assured of all the days of my life.

Truth #2: I am never alone.

"No one will be able to stand against you all the days of your life. As I was with Moses, so I will be with you; I will never leave you nor forsake you" (Joshua 1:5).

My relationship and companionship with Jesus has sustained me. I know that when my heart was broken, His heart was broken too. When no one else understands, the Creator of my very heart does and he sends the Comforter, the Holy Spirit, to help me.

When fearful, isolated, or rejected, I remember the suffering that my Savior endured, the lashes, the crown of thorns, the curses, the nails driven through flesh and bone — wounds that understand my pain — and the thought of His love for me makes me whole again, connects me to Him, and turns my fears into faith.

Growing up without a biological father and with an abusive stepfather, I had a very difficult time relating to God as my Heavenly Father. I almost cringed at the word "father," as it conjured up negative feelings. It took many years of learning the nature of God, the attributes of God, the names of God, believing the promises of God, and understanding the great mystery, the Trinity. The Trinity—God my father, Jesus my Savior, and the Holy Spirit my comforter are eternal, and will never leave me or forsake me.

In 2006, I attended a Christian retreat called Tres Dias, three days with God. On that retreat, themes of God our Father, God our daddy, penetrated my heart and broke down my distaste for the word "father," "daddy," and reversed the image of an overbearing, tyrant-type father, into a loving, compassionate, caring Father, God—a Father whom I was secure in knowing would never leave me or forsake me.

**Truth #3: God knows me
intimately and made me for kingdom purpose.**

"For you created my inmost being; you knit me together in my mother's womb. I praise you because I am fearfully and wonderfully made; your works are

wonderful, I know that full well. My frame was not hidden from you when I was made in the secret place, when I was woven together in the depths of the earth. Your eyes saw my unformed body; all the days ordained for me were written in your book before one of them came to be. How precious to me are your thoughts, God! How vast is the sum of them! Were I to count them, they would outnumber the grains of sand— when I awake, I am still with you" (Psalm 139:13–18).

The God who created the heavens and earth created me intimately. The psalmist praises God's handiwork in Psalm 139 by saying God created them intentionally, and they are "fearfully and wonderfully made." Not only am I God's masterpiece, but God has a special purpose for my life that spans the number of my days. The psalmist continues, "Your eyes saw my unformed body; all the days ordained for me were written in your book before one of them came to be." My existence is no mistake; my mission here on earth is no mistake. I was destined before time began to be on the earth at this exact time.

I often hear the question, "Why does God let

bad things happen? Especially to children?"
Well, we live in a fallen world where Satan rules
and reigns, but God created man to have free will.
I don't believe God causes bad things to happen.
My abuse came from the decision of a man to
abuse me, under evil persuasion. However, God
can take what was meant for evil and use it to
turn it into something good for His glory and
purposes.

> *"And we know that all things work
> together for good to those who love God, to
> those who are called according to His
> purpose" (Romans 8:28).*

We all have purpose here on earth. My name,
"Angela," means messenger of God. God wired
me to be tenacious and willing to fight for what is
right and just. He gave me talents and skills as a
communicator, both written and oral. He also
gave me compassion to understand the needs of
those who have suffered. I can think of no greater
calling than to share how God took the painful
experiences of my life and turned them to a
ministry to fight against the evil of abuse and help
in healing for those who are hurting. He knows
me intimately and has a good plan for my life.

Truth #4: I am who God says I am.

We are special in God's eyes. God has a special plan for my life and yours. After abuse has taken our spark, we don't always feel very special. We feel quite the opposite: flawed, inferior. But *not* in God's eyes. Whenever insecurities rear their ugly head, I turn to the truth in scripture. I quiet my spirit and listen to God's still, small voice within:

> *"Do not fear for I have redeemed you; I have summoned you by name; you are mine . . ." (Isaiah 43:1).*

God continues a few verses later:

> *"Since you are precious and honored in my sight, and because I love you . . ." (Isaiah 43:4)*

Imagine the Lord saying that to you. Insecurities cannot rob you of who you are unless you let them.

I am the apple of God's eye.

> *"For thus says the Lord of hosts: 'He sent Me after glory, to the nations which plunder you; for he who touches you touches the apple of His eye'" (Zechariah 2:8).*

He sings over me:

> *"The Lord your God in your midst, The*
> *Mighty One, will save; He will rejoice over*
> *you with gladness, He will quiet you with*
> *His love, He will rejoice over you with*
> *singing" (Zephaniah 3:17).*

I am who God says I am and as bright as my spark shines on the outside, the spark should shine as bright on the inside.

Truth #5: God has a good plan for my life.

> *"'For I know the plans I have for you,' says*
> *the Lord, 'plans to prosper you and not to*
> *harm you, plans to give you hope and a*
> *future'" (Jeremiah 29:11).*

Our world is full of brokenness and sin, but God offers hope and restoration. God's plan for my life offers hope and a prosperous future, where I can thrive beyond my wildest dreams. There are many ways that God wants to bless us.

The psalmist exclaims:

> *"Praise the Lord, O my soul, and forget*
> *not all his benefits – who forgives all your*

sins and heals all your diseases, who redeems your life from the pit and crowns you with love and compassion, who satisfies your desires with good things so that your youth is renewed like the eagle's" (Psalm 103:1–5).

God desires my healing, renewal, and restoration. God not only wishes to bless me, He has big dreams for my life if I only follow Him in obedience. And in that obedience, we will reap a rich harvest.

"And let us not grow weary while doing good, for in due season we shall reap if we do not lose heart" (Galatians 6:9).

Even when challenges come, I have to continue to trust God. Even when I face rejection, I have learned that life's rejection is often God's protection.

Truth #6: I have a special strength available through my faith: the Power of Jesus Christ.

This is my all-time favorite verse that brings me strength, and I repeat it often:

"I can do all things through Christ, who strengthens me" (Philippians 4:13).

At the darkest moment of my life, when I had tried repeatedly on January 16, 1983, to take my own life, at the very end of my rope, God spoke these words to me. I had no idea where to go or what to do at three a.m. — cold, barefoot, lonely, and hopeless — but these words came to me.

God was with me in that moment of desperation, and He intervened. He gave me the strength and the power to put one foot in front of the other and He led me to safety that night.

Be assured that the God who has numbered the hairs on your head is fighting for you. His favor will surround you like a shield.

*"For You, O Lord, will bless the righteous;
With favor You will surround him as with
a shield" (Psalm 5:12).*

We have an insurmountable ally in our God — for if God is for us, who can be against us?

**Truth #7: God hears my prayers
and can move mountains on my behalf.**

Prayer changes things. Jesus reiterates the

power of prayer in scripture, especially when we pray using His name.

> *"Jesus says, 'And I will do whatever you ask in my name, so that the Father may be glorified in the Son. You may ask me for anything in my name, and I will do it'"* (John 14:13–14).

While I can't control God's answer to my prayers, prayer opens the door for God to act through my faith. I know God hears my prayers, and every time I pray, I experience peace.

Paul writes:

> *"Do not be anxious about anything, but in every situation, by prayer and petition, with thanksgiving, present your requests to God. And the peace of God, which transcends all understanding, will guard your hearts and your minds in Christ Jesus"* (Philippians 4:6–7).

I am always amazed that I can meet with the Creator of the universe in prayer and know that I have His ear and He meets me right where I am. Sometimes, I don't even know what to pray about so I just sit in silence or pray in the spirit.

God created us for communion with Him so I believe He is pleased to hear my prayers and receive my worship. If you, too, don't know how to pray, just invite God into that moment and just seek Him.

> *"Draw near to God and He will draw near to you"* *(James 4:8)*

Prayer brings me peace, strengthens my faith, and prayer is a power source to draw closer to God.

Truth #8: Hope is always alive in my life through faith.

Creation is groaning, and hope is hard to find some days in the devastation of the world—storms, wars, evil, abuse, lies, deception, senseless violence, both heartbreaking and worsening, so many evil forces that could cause us to lose hope. And we are not immune to loss or hurt in our personal life.

I have experienced much pain in my life. I'm sad to say that I did face a moment of hopelessness, where I could not see a path forward. I am so grateful that I now have the maturity to deal with those spirals. We are human and we will face dark days, but we must always turn to the light. When I hear the whispers of Satan, the what-if thoughts, the doubt creeps in and I am tempted to lose hope, but I remind myself of the scripture's promise:

> *"Those who sow with tears will reap with songs of joy"* (Psalm 126:5).

When I'm sad, Jesus reminds me that He is with those who mourn.

> *"Blessed are those who mourn, For they shall be comforted"* (Matthew 5:4).

Fear is a big part of my bout with hopelessness. I once learned that FEAR is *False Evidence Appearing Real*. I have found that if I travel the road of fear to the worst possible outcome, then I can figure out a solution from there because I trust God and His plan for my life. Loving me is living free of fear and full of faith.

> *"For God has not given us a spirit of fear, but of power and of love and of a sound mind"* (2 Timothy 1:7).

Joyce Meyer, a wise woman, has said, "If you

are afraid to conquer a task, just do it AFRAID."
No matter how dire my situation, I know my God
can bring beauty out of ashes — even death does
not have the last word.

> *"For God so loved the world that he gave
> his one and only Son, that whoever
> believes in him shall not perish but have
> eternal life" (John 3:16).*

Our hope is eternal; when our work on earth is
done, we will be with God forever.

> *"Let not your heart be troubled; you
> believe in God, believe also in Me. In My
> Father's house are many mansions; if it
> were not so, I would have told you. I go to
> prepare a place for you. And if I go and
> prepare a place for you, I will come again
> and receive you to Myself; that where I am,
> there you may be also" (John 14:1–3).*

Hope and faith go hand in hand. Neither we
can see, but by commitment we believe. Many
lead with their flesh — they depend on how they
feel. I lead with my heart, and I trust God. In
doing so over and over, my muscle of faith is
strengthened.

"Now faith is confidence in what we hope for and assurance about what we do not see" (Hebrews 11:1).

Faith can work powerfully in your life as well to empower you to live in peace, experience an abundance of joy, and dream big. To receive hope, Jesus encourages us to adopt the innocent, trusting nature of a child.

"Jesus said, 'Let the little children come to me, and do not hinder them, for the kingdom of heaven belongs to such as these'" (Matthew 19:14).

It truly breaks my heart when children are abused because they have blind faith in goodness. That gives us cause to praise and remain hope filled. Paul encourages us:

"Whatever things are true, whatever things are noble, whatever things are just, whatever things are pure, whatever things are lovely, whatever things are of good report, if there is any virtue and if there is anything praiseworthy – meditate on these things" (Philippians 4:8).

Never stop flexing your faith muscle and, believe me, it will grow.

Truth #9: God reveals Himself to me through scripture, prayer, and the body of believers.

No person is perfect, no church is perfect, but we serve a perfect God. Through the grace of Jesus Christ, we can reflect Christ when we empty ourselves of our own agendas and seek God's path. We can be the hands and feet of Jesus in the lives of others, and they, too, can pour into our lives. Pivotal moments of my faith have been ushered in through other believers. Jesus underlines the power of community when he states:

> *"For where two or three gather in my name, there am I with them" (Matthew 18:20).*

We find God in fellowship with one another, and God reveals himself as we worship in community. We can also accomplish the work of the church.

> *"The Spirit of the Sovereign Lord is on me because the Lord has anointed me to*

proclaim good news to the poor. He has sent me to bind up the brokenhearted, to proclaim freedom for the captives and release from darkness for the prisoners...to comfort all who mourn . . ." (Isaiah 61:1–2)

When we serve in ways like this, in Jesus's name, we receive supernatural power, we give flesh to the spiritual promises that we benefit from and believe in, and we have the opportunity to share them with the world — that is love! When I love like Jesus, I love myself even more.

There are many more truths I cling to from scripture, and I encourage you to dive in and make your own list of the truths you will embrace to guide your life. As I strive to live by these truths, they empower me to be the Angela I aspire to be.

Recently, my mom started calling me "radiant," which has been a huge compliment because that is what I aspire to be consistently. I want to radiate Jesus. I want to have such a bright presence that it can't help but draw others closer to the cross. We have never arrived, as there is always room to grow on this journey of life.

I once heard that if you are not growing, you're dying, and that God created every living thing to grow. From glory to glory — that is where I want to grow. Whether I've had a good day or a bad day, whether I've failed or succeeded, whether I'm a size six or sixteen, whether I have imperfections in my appearance or a perfect smile, I want to give more love to the woman in the mirror so she can, in turn, pour out that love to others.

CHAPTER 3

Loving My Life

"This day I call the heavens and the earth as witnesses against you that I have set before you life and death, blessings and curses. Now choose life, so that you and your children may live and that you may love the LORD your God, listen to his voice, and hold fast to him. For the LORD is your life, and he will give you many years in the land he swore to give to your fathers, Abraham, Isaac and Jacob" *(Deuteronomy 30:19–20).*

As I mentioned before, I considered and

attempted taking my life more than once. I didn't want to die—I just wanted the suffering to end. For many years, as a child and into young adulthood, the thought of death consumed me and, finally, overwhelmed me.

My first attempt, though harmless, was in third grade when I swallowed the contents of an entire bottle of vitamin A. It was the only bottle I could get the top off.

At my most desperate time, I almost succeeded at age seventeen. I truly believe God intervened, and when you read the following excerpt from my first memoir, *From Sorrows to Sapphires*, you will agree. It was not my time, for He had a better life for me to live, more love for me to experience, more adventure for me to embark on, more Kingdom business that He equipped me to accomplish. I share my despair to encourage you that your darkest moments may become your brightest beginning.

I revisit the day I attempted suicide with grief for my younger self who lost all hope in humanity and the sacredness of life. I hurt for so long that I just wanted the pain to end. It was Sunday, January 16, 1983—the beginning of the end—a day that changed my life forever, a day I can never forget, no matter how hard as I try.

There had been great turmoil in our home that day — lots of cursing, screaming, and berating.

I don't know if it was a panic attack or just a break from reality, but something snapped inside my psyche. I sat frozen on a swing in our backyard, repeating the words "It's over." I methodically planned my suicide, taking every step in my mind.

First, retrieve the bottle of vodka under the kitchen sink, grab the checkbook in the drawer to purchase the sleeping pills, find the keys to the car on the kitchen counter. And at dark-thirty, my mother would be fast asleep, and I would make my getaway. As I sat on that swing, tears streaming down my face, my mind walked through the steps of the suicide plan. Dark settled and the temperature dropped.

Barefoot and wearing only a T-shirt and jeans, I walked surefootedly into the kitchen, retrieved the items from my list, rolled the car down the driveway, and cranked it, off to do the deed.

It was pitch-black around 9:30 p.m., and I parked the car in the remote woods near my high school. I turned the radio up, tore the seal off the first bottle of sleeping pills, and began to wash them down with the vodka — one after another as fast as I could. I ripped off the seal of the second bottle with my teeth and slammed a handful in my mouth.

I could feel my body become like lead as it became difficult to move my arms or legs, and my mouth was so dry, but all I had was the vodka. My eyes grew heavy, and my head swam. I felt myself sinking into the white bucket seats and felt it would be a peaceful departure.

I began to pray for forgiveness for this act because I knew this was wrong, but I consoled myself that I had no other choice.

I woke up hours later on the cold dirt, having rolled out of the car and onto the ground while violently vomiting. When I retrieved my composure, all I could do was scream. I had failed; I was alive and had no idea what to do.

The night went on forever with two other attempts. I climbed to the top of the Talmage Bridge and looked into the cold black water but couldn't let go. I drove over the bridge on the wrong side of the road, inviting a head-on collision, but when I peaked the top of the bridge, I only had flashes of harming someone else.

Cold, hopeless, and helpless, I sat on the side of the road and just shook my head. It was a long and arduous climb back to life, but my life was given back to me that night by the mercy and grace of God even though I couldn't live another moment in the abuse. God had the steps of my escape planned for me.

Please believe me when I say that I am extremely sorry I attempted to take my own life, but I am eternally grateful God spared me on that hopeless and desperate night. I share the darkest moments of my life, when I lost all hope, to help others see there is a better way, a better day.

I am so sorry for those of you reading my words who have also contemplated suicide. I understand. Our world has so many people hurting from past trauma, yet so few places to heal. Our families — well, most want to sweep any dirty laundry under the rug and chase us around and around the dysfunction mountain. But sometimes we are blessed to have a close family member, friend, or spouse to walk us through the healing. Unfortunately, and oftentimes, our pain puts a strain on those relationships. Therapy is another solution, but mental health counseling is usually not covered by insurance, making therapy costly, time consuming, and challenging when finding the right therapist.

We may hope the church would be that safe place to heal, that certainly is what Jesus wanted. But unfortunately, this issue is taxing, overwhelming, and most are scared to get their hands dirty because it's hard. Consequently, we stuff our pain until we explode. When we explode, we usually blow up on those closest to us. We may attempt to heal in isolation, but rarely does this approach work. We end up spiraling out of control.

For those who have not reached those depths of despair, I'm sure it is difficult to comprehend that moment when you lose all hope and believe the whispers of, "The world would just be better off without me," or "I have no other choice," or "I just want the suffering to end." Sound familiar? A constant whisper becomes a roar. If you are battling those thoughts, I ask that you stop reading and reach out to someone—a pastor, a friend, a counselor, or a help line.

God loves you and wants you to live an abundant joyful life. I believe the Word of God and the truth about life:

> "For you created my inmost being; you knit me together in my mother's womb. I praise you because I am fearfully and wonderfully made; your works are wonderful, I know that full well. My frame was not hidden from you when I was made in the secret place, when I was woven together in the depths of the earth. Your

*eyes saw my unformed body; all the days
ordained for me were written in your book
before one of them came to be. How
precious to me are your thoughts, God!
How vast is the sum of them! Were I to
count them, they would outnumber the
grains of sand — when I awake, I am still
with you" (Psalm 139:13–18).*

I believe that my days and your days were
ordained before time began, and my name and
your name was written in the Lamb's Book of
Life. I believe His plan for our lives — His plan for
me to live out my days on this earth with
abundant love, joy, peace, passion, and destiny. I
know beyond a shadow of a doubt that God was
with me on that horrible night and saved my life.
I believe if you are suffering, God is with you,
waiting for you to cry out to Him.

*"For there is no difference between Jew and
Gentile — the same Lord is Lord of all and
richly blesses all who call on him, for,
'Everyone who calls on the name of the
Lord will be saved'" (Romans 10:12–14).*

I have felt from the time I was very young that
my life had destiny beyond what I could

understand. I felt the Holy Spirit at a very young age as I was being brutally beaten and worse. I could escape the attacks in my mind. While my body was fully present, I learned to go elsewhere in my mind.

My heart hurts for any child violated in such a ripping of innocence. But for many years, I did not have compassion for that little girl who was me. I had to learn to have compassion for the little girl crying inside of me. I had to learn to love her. She was frozen in time, frozen in pain, waiting to be thawed by the warmth of love and rescued by forgiveness.

I struggled for so many years feeling like I would never be at peace, never heal, and that the world would be better off without me. What an incredible lie. That little girl needed compassion and understanding that the abuse was never her fault. She needed the inner battle and blame to end.

It's difficult to explain but the moment I set her free, the moment I stopped punishing her, my healing progressed. I figuratively sat her on my lap and gave her a hug. If I could not love her, the one who suffered, how could I love life? We are a compilation of every day we have ever lived. It's like a tree — when cut down, we see the rings of its life, one on top of the other, each ring strengthening the next. That is our life: one ring after another of every experience, wrapping around our soul.

I ask you, right now, to please quiet your thoughts. Imagine your younger self, perhaps the age when you were first abused. You can imagine with your eyes closed or find a photo. Think of the age your abuse first began. Think of how you looked, what you were wearing, the smells of the room. At that moment in time, you were innocent. Though painful, traumatizing, even paralyzing, know that Jesus was there. Know He grieves for you and grieves with you. Give yourself this moment to share your thoughts and maybe give your younger self a huge hug, forgiveness, a break, some form of compassion.

Today, when I see a three-year-old—the age I was when my abuse began—I can hardly breathe. I see that helpless child and know there was no way I could have stopped my abuser, no way I could have defended myself. In that moment, I extend as much love and grace to that little one who just needed protection. What cuts deep is the adults who surrounded me looked the other way. If you see or sense abuse, please don't look the other way. Be the hero in that child's life—intervene, seek help, and report the abuse.

My life has been incredibly fruitful, blessed beyond measure. I love my life. I have managed, by the grace of God, to have a wonderful marriage to the love of my life, Phillip Williams, for almost forty years. I have birthed two amazing human beings—both frontline workers, sacrificially giving of themselves daily. Both have limitless courage and sacrifice their lives for others—that is love. That is the legacy I am leaving behind. My heart explodes with love, with pride for the two amazing adults they have become. I have also been blessed to have touched many lives with the message of healing, and I pray this book continues that legacy.

I love my life and never again will I let the thoughts of suicide creep in. I challenge you to take inventory of your life and all that you have to love about yourself and your life.

CHAPTER 4

Loving Others

"A new command I give you: Love one another. As I have loved you, so you must love one another" (John 13:34).

Though I realize all who meet me may not love me, I've come to accept that it's really okay, because I have an empowering, all-encompassing love for myself. I could not have said that years ago. I was such a people pleaser that it devastated me if someone didn't like me. I had a real problem with rejection.

I have been so blessed to learn to not only love myself unconditionally but to love others, releasing ulterior motives and expectations. In my more mature years, I have learned that expectations set me up for disappointment, because it's difficult for others to meet my expectations, let alone even comprehend what I expect from them.

Every child yearns to have a father to love them. I yearned for it my whole life. The greatest rejection I have faced is from my biological father, who walked away from me as an infant and never looked back. For so long, I chased a dream of a heartfelt reunion with my biological father. He has lived an hour from me from age zero to eighteen and then less than five hours from eighteen on. Several times I have reached out, desiring some kind of connection, and the repeated rejection was depleting. Somehow, I let my stepfather's words, "Your own father never wanted you," penetrate my heart. I had to come face-to-face with the reality of his hurtful words.

It has all been overwhelming at times, yet I fight the tears that would say my abuser was right and stay strong. I have reconciled this defeat by accepting that my father not embracing his fatherhood or me has nothing to do with me and everything to do with him and his capacity to love. It is difficult for me to understand that decision, but I have come to terms with this void in my life and laid down any expectations of my father.

When I was wallowing in the wounding, I could not truly love others nor could I truly allow them to love me. I had built such thick walls around my heart because so many people who touted they loved me but ended up hurting me. I lumped all people in a pile of the untrusted. You might not hurt me today or tomorrow, but I was waiting, because I knew, one day soon, you would hurt me.

So I just kept everyone at bay. I even kept my precious husband at bay for the first few years of our marriage. I regret my actions, reacting from a place of pain. I even tortured the poor man, thinking to myself, *I know I will eventually push the right button and prove myself right, and he will flee.* It took a lot of arguing and a lot of dysfunction before he screamed at the top of his lungs, "I am never going to leave you! I love you, and we can either be miserable or happy—your choice!" At the publishing of this book, we have been happily married for almost forty years.

When he hammered down the walls around my heart, I surrendered my whole heart on a platter. Our relationship has sweetened with every passing year. I love him so much it hurts some days. I drive down our long and winding driveway every day and say, "Thank you, God, for that precious man who loves me so well," and can't wait to return home at the end of the workday. When I surrendered, we were in Fiji. We were at a self-care conference and connected like never before. On that little island that was filled with so much love and spirit, I was able to process through the distrust and be accountable for my bad behavior.

I also had a very difficult time communicating my true feelings. Part of being so numb and so silent for a long time is you begin to mask your true self, your true feelings. Phil got so tired of hearing me say, "I'm fine," when he would ask how I was feeling. He suspected pain was present. The truth of the matter is I was not fine but I had to hold it together. I spent a lot of energy keeping it together and holding the floodgates closed on my emotions. I always share that I had to have a breakdown in order to have a breakthrough. I guess I was always so terrified of the breakdown that I postponed doing the heavy lifting of healing. The most important step was, and still is, being vulnerable to share my struggles.

If I could change one day of my life, I wouldn't. I was in the heart of my healing, really making great strides, and then it was as if God said, "I am going to expedite your healing here and now." I was able to release so much that I had been holding on to so tightly. Phil and my relationship began to change. Our passion began to intensify, our love strengthened, and our marriage enriched. He is truly my soul mate and knows me better than I know myself. I realize what a blessing it is to be married to my soul mate, my best friend, and greatest confidant. The safest, most secure place in the world is in his arms, listening to him say, "I love you," as I fall asleep. All is well with the world.

Phil has always shown an amazing, uncon-ditional, all-encompassing, all-forgiving love for me. He says he lives to make me happy and my happiness is the most important focus in his life. His actions speak even louder than his words, as I truly feel cherished. I pray for that kind of sacrificial, pure, transparent, passionate love for you if you are seeking a soul mate. Don't settle. If you do not have that special someone in your life at present, know that God has an abundant love for you that will also help you grow to love yourself after abuse. If you do have a special someone in your life, allow that love to help you heal.

Phil's love has been a great source of healing. It has forgiven my faults, compromised through struggles, shared my dreams, cared for me, respected me, and offered an abundance of mercy and patience. His passion and pure love have helped me release the shame of my abuse.

I challenge you, if you are struggling in your marriage today, to take inventory of your relationship. Do you have walls built around your heart? Do you struggle to communicate your true feelings? Do you have trust issues that need to be resolved? Do you keep people at bay in fear of being hurt again? Is God first in your marriage? Or maybe, you are in a relationship with the wrong person, perhaps even caught in the cycle of repeated abuse. It might be time to take inventory and make some tough decisions to protect yourself and stop the cycle of abuse in your life.

God puts people in our lives to teach us how to love and how to be loved. I believe people are in our lives for a reason, a season, or a lifetime. Only time will tell. Lifetime people are obviously family and those close friends who you enjoy spending time with. We all know who those people are: The ones whom God knits our hearts together and we do life together. The people in our lives who bring us an abundance of joy, make us smile, who root for us and you for them, who would meet us in the middle of the night, no questions asked, if only you were to utter the words, "I need you." Those relationships are so few, so precious, so genuine, and so absolutely, incredibly comforting. To know I am not alone is a healing ointment to my hurts and wraps me in love.

Our instinct when we are the "walking wounded" is to isolate. That is *not* the path to healing. You may have to take a leap of faith on these words, but as much as you want to insulate and isolate, we must open our hearts for these genuine relationships to flourish. Consider opening your mind and your heart to the person knocking at your door.

The person I had the least in common with became my dearest friend, because she gave me what I lacked and I gave her what she missed. Her name was Polly Moore, and she was forever grateful to me for traveling with her on her healing journey from child sexual abuse. I will be forever grateful to her for giving me the most innocent, genuine, and encouraging of friendships.

For over a decade, we continued to pour into each other's lives, sharing our lives. She shared experiences I had never known, and I introduced her to experiences she had only dreamed of. We were like *Mutt and Jeff* and we never had a moment when we weren't laughing and living life.

I will never forget her words, "I am here for you, Angela Williams." And she was always there for me, through thick and thin, ups and downs, mountains and valleys. Polly Moore was my dearest friend, and I will miss her forever and a day, but I know I will see her again in heaven. She passed away from a long battle with autoimmune disease and liver failure in 2022. She often said it was the abuse that poisoned her body.

Polly was in my life for a reason and a season, to show me true friendship and help me fight the good fight of advocacy, and she loved me so much; she made me love me MOORE. If you haven't read the dedication yet, please circle back.

I would be remiss if I didn't talk about how challenging our family relationships can be. My biological father was not the only hard relationship in my life. Honestly, family can sometimes be the most difficult relationships in our lives. We don't get to choose our family, and some family dynamics can be riddled with dysfunction. They are in our lives (if we chose) for a lifetime.

Unfortunately, our family can't love us the way we want or need to be loved. I have come to terms with these challenges and have grown to learn that sometimes family loves us the only way they know how. They can only love us with the tools in their toolbox. If they have never been taught compassion, they may struggle to give compassion. Their guilt or personal trauma may prevent them from truly investing in the relationship. And of course, there may be cycles of abuse, selfishness, resentment, envy, jealousy, anger, and judgment in the family that are never broken and that they struggle to heal.

Our fences (defenses) may keep others at bay for fear we may get hurt. Yes, God forbid, we may get hurt. Let me assure you, we *are* going to be hurt. Our feelings are tender; our threshold is shallow. But we must take the hits in stride, knowing we have to process the hurt in a healthy manner.

We live in such a fleshly, secular, wicked world, it's inevitable we will experience disappointment, rejection, grief—and it will hurt. Some of our hurt, I believe, is malicious and some, I believe, is directed from Satan to divert our destiny. But God will make sure, though we may be derailed, we will not be overcome. God puts people in our lives for a reason, a season, or a lifetime.

> *"These things I have spoken to you, that in Me you may have peace. In the world you will have tribulation; but be of good cheer, I have overcome the world" (John 16:33).*

I was deeply wounded in May of 2017 when the organization I founded to help abuse survivors, was ripped from my hands by a hostile takeover by the board of directors, believing they could do better and that I was not the right leader for the organization. As if that wasn't enough pain, they made false accusations and tried to ruin my reputation. I was betrayed by people I deeply trusted with my dreams. It was terribly painful, and I grieved the loss. And new grief brings back the pain of old grief. I grieved for many months, but I knew I had to heal to continue the work God has called me to accomplish.

This book is my first attempt to dip my toes back into the water. God planted this book in my heart shortly after it happened, but I just couldn't write it. I think I was grieving (and pouting), and let's face it, more times than not, life gets in the way of being obedient to God. I am so grateful that I serve a patient God that allowed me to truly heal before standing back up and stepping back into ministry. For those of you in ministry, you will understand, but full-time ministry brings an all-out spiritual attack. If you are doing good in the Kingdom God, you are in Satan's crosshairs.

I'm taking a leap of faith with no preconceived expectations and pray I land where I'm destined to be. I believe that the magnitude of perseverance isn't measured by time but consistency and unwavering faith.

> *"'For I know the plans I have for you,' declares the Lord, 'plans to prosper you and not to harm you, plans to give you hope and a future'" (Jeremiah 29:11).*

When we are wounded again, it's easy to pick up all the old baggage of pain and heap it on our shoulders again like a badge of honor. If we realize our current state of grief often taps into those previous scars of grief, then we tend to relive past pain. Grief comes in waves. It doesn't mean you are doing anything wrong. Feel it, breathe through it, and come back to your center, the here and now, and pray.

I remember, in the depth of my pain, I could

be doing something simple like vacuuming and break down in a flood of tears. I have learned to deal with the struggle at hand instead of stuffing it down for another day. God is here now to give us the healing and victory we need. God will give us peace. He promises peace and rest for our soul.

> *"Take My yoke upon you and learn from Me, for I am gentle and lowly in heart, and you will find rest for your souls. For My yoke is easy and My burden is light"* (Matthew 11:29–30).

Sometimes it is easier, or by habit, to play the victim card than to do the hard work of healing. The victim card is a free pass to live in torment and turmoil, depressed, to revert to bad behaviors and keep the cycle of abuse going because "people who are suffering hurt other people." Not only for our own sake but for the sake of those that love us, we must do the hard work of healing so we can foster healthy relationships.

Unintentionally, our pain spills over into other people's lives, often the people we love the most, who are closest to us. Letting go of the pain doesn't happen all at once. It bears repeating that healing is a process, not a destination. It happens little by little so we must be patient and gentle with ourselves. I keep laying my pain before the throne of Jesus and asking God what He would have me do.

When my work of ten years was ripped from my hands, I laid my pain before Jesus and I was told, very audibly, to sit down, not to defend myself, and that He would fight my battles. My fleshly nature is not to sit down and be quiet; my nature is to fight like hell, tooth and nail.

Those who know me well know that I have a passionate determination, with the most infuriating trigger for me being the abuse of children. As hard as it was to not fight back, I reluctantly obeyed and laid down the ministry work. I've been on the sidelines now for five years. That's a long time to put a dream on a shelf. But if I truly trust God, I must trust His perfect timing to stand up.

One of my challenges in life is waiting. I am a type-A, where-there-is-a-will-there-is-a-way doer. I was hurt and feeling like the hard work of ten years was destroyed. In retrospect, I was a vessel being used by God, as the ministry was not mine, it was His. I needed this time to truly listen to God, because God's plans and purposes for this world are far bigger, broader, and deeper than my small part of it. This is God's story.

My husband always says, "People live their lives trying to fit God into their story versus seeking how they fit into God's story." We are but a small blip on God's timeline. If we understand how our lives are meant to impact others in God's timeline — if we love ourselves as we love others and engage — then we are a ripple in the big pond of life, and that ripple can impact people who impact others and even alter the trajectory of a single life or family for generations. Your life may be a ripple, a wave, or a tsunami, and you may not even realize your impact, this side of heaven.

God wants to use our mess and turn it into a message.

> *"They triumphed over him by the blood of the Lamb and by the word of their testimony; they did not love their lives so much as to shrink from death" (Revelation 12:11).*

As we let our walls down and begin to trust again, accepting we may be hurt in these future relationships is vital to our social and mental health. The risk of being hurt is just a part of this life. Fostering healthy, intimate, close relationships is worth the risk, especially if we are healed and can understand how to process future hurt. I'm not saying the future wounds will be easy, but the strength that we gain from overcoming abuse will help us heal more quickly and more easily. We will have wounds, but they won't cut as deep as the scars of the past.

I believe hurt teaches us a lot about ourselves and about others. If we can pause before we react, dissect the sting, express our true feelings, we can strengthen our communication skills and reconcile these hurts in a healthy way by sharing the depth of our feelings. We can evaluate how the pain impacts the relationship. Is the other person quick to say, "I'm sorry" or "I understand how you feel," or do they get defensive and blame or judge you for your feelings?

Healthy relationships are challenging. There are motives, agendas, feelings, and a struggle to understand perspectives. Wisdom, discernment, and boundaries are muscles that need to be strengthened to know how to proceed and discern whether the relationship is healthy or not. Sometimes we just need time to pray for wisdom and discernment to have Godly guidance in our response.

"My dear brothers and sisters, take note of this: Everyone should be quick to listen, slow to speak and slow to become angry, because human anger does not produce the righteousness that God desires" (James 1:19–20).

This has been a hard lesson for me to learn—to be slow to speak—but one that has served me well. More times than not, when I am quick to speak, I often regret the words that part my lips. Words can never be unsaid, taken back, or forgotten. After spending so many years in silence, while never being able to defend myself, once I got my voice, I used it unsparingly. It's been a difficult lesson to learn, but thinking before I speak, or just being silent, is one that has made me a better person.

Forming good boundaries keeps our relationships healthy. I heard once that walls are our emotions and the door is the boundary. We can choose who enters our life. We are complicated beings—easily influenced, distracted, overwhelmed, with so much competition for our time and attention. I believe wisdom has everything to do with taking the time to put God first in every decision and living our life for an audience of one, while discerning outside influences. You can never

please everyone, but we can please God by
seeking Him and His ways, always—making time
to pray, room to listen, and the discipline to obey.
If there is confusion, sometimes we just need to
wait and seek wise counsel.

> *"If any of you lacks wisdom, you should
> ask God, who gives generously to all
> without finding fault, and it will be given
> to you"* (James 1:5).

Discernment is a gift of spiritual guidance and
understanding. A synonym is perception.

I envy my husband, Phil; he has great
discernment. He can meet a person and read their
spirit within seconds. He can weed through a
situation, get to the heart of the matter quickly,
and offer a solution. Discernment is that gut
check to go right or left, to stand up or sit down,
to speak or be silent, to run or walk, to engage or
not. It's tough.

All these decisions determine our destiny.
Good boundaries that protect our heart are more
difficult because we have to possess great
wisdom and discernment to know where to draw
the boundary lines. People in our lives either
understand and respect boundaries or they don't.

Those who don't respect our value, body, time, or wishes are unhealthy, toxic.

Toxic people are self-absorbed, narcissistic, and the most challenging relationships in our life. It's okay to walk away from toxic people. Sometimes, our family is the most likely to disrespect us and are often offended by our boundaries, putting their needs first.

It took me a very long time to accept that it's okay to say no. It's okay to end a call when it becomes unhealthy. It's okay to walk away. It's okay to refrain from events that may be painful, and it's okay to put my physical and mental health first.

I attended my paternal grandparents' funerals knowing I would have a very awkward encounter with my biological father, but I went anyway. It was not as bad as I imagined, but painful nonetheless. Loving yourself means protecting yourself. I love me enough to protect me and not subject myself to toxic people or toxic situations unless I choose. I chose to go, and I chose to limit my interaction with my father, and I had the support of my husband and children.

There will always be challenging people in our life who are difficult to love, who are dealing with their own dysfunction and disorders. These personality disorders can range from master manipulators, passive aggressiveness, codependency to narcissism, to ultimately abusiveness.

The master manipulator is a person who controls or influences others in a clever or abusive behavior. Passive aggressive behavior is characterized by passive hostility and negative behavior through actions instead of communicating the hostility directly. Codependent behavior is someone who exhibits excessive reliance or emotional dependence on another, where one person is entirely responsible for meeting another person's needs—so much so that they can't function independently. A narcissist is someone who has extreme self-involvement, self-importance, excessive vanity, and is self-centered to the point that they ignore the needs of others, lacking empathy and compassion. Abusive behavior is a pattern of abusive and coercive behaviors used to maintain power and control that can be verbal, emotional, physical, or sexual. Abusive relationships are often accompanied by violence and fear of violence.

Can you identify these unhealthy behaviors in any of your relationships?

This is why we must love, accept, and trust ourselves, so that we will be confident in identifying and dealing with unhealthy relationships. We are worth defending.

Oftentimes, when you confront a manipulator about what they did wrong, they will blame you. Standing up is frightening, especially if your abuser is physically or verbally abusive, and you risk retaliation. Put safety first—have someone with you when you confront your abuser. If confrontation could be met with violence, then you might consider terminating the relationship. I realize that is easier said than done.

Frequently, we love the ones who hurt us the most. We always believe that their behavior will change or we take it upon ourselves to attempt to change them. Sometimes, we doubt ourselves. When we doubt our feelings, push them aside, and tell ourselves, "Oh, they didn't treat me so badly; I must have done something to provoke it," or, "I shouldn't have overreacted," we are giving in to the manipulation and abandoning our true selves.

I heard from my mother, many times, after the violent bouts of abuse that, "he didn't mean it; he didn't hit you hard, you'll be fine." When we accept this life, we are reverting back to that abused, soul-seeking approval and love. It's okay to stand up for yourself. Own your response in a situation, but make sure you communicate that the other person *must* own their behavior, otherwise there can be no honest, healthy, or helpful resolution. If you cherish the relationship and don't seek resolution, unresolved issues fester and will more than likely escalate. You deserve to be seen, heard, respected, and loved, and without resolution, nothing will change.

Did I mention relationships are hard?

As I've said before, and you may read again, "people who are suffering hurt people." That is why healing is so critical for me and for those I touch. When someone is aching, they bleed on you too. You will never ease your pain by striking out on those around you. Though not always easy, we are called to forgive . . . ourselves and others.

One of the most difficult yet freeing stages of my healing was forgiving myself. So often I blamed myself for not telling someone, anyone, about my abuse. I felt so trapped and defenseless. I also felt responsible for the safety of my mother and my siblings. My stepfather always threatened hurting my mother if I ever told. I was always in a catch-22, damned either way.

Obviously, it was difficult to forgive my abuser and all those who had abandoned me, neglected me, turned a blind eye to my suffering. I also was mad at God. Somewhere deep inside, I asked, "Why, God? Why was I abused, suffering then and now?" I don't know the answer to that question. But what I do know is I've learned that forgiveness is not a feeling but an act of obedience. I realized I was seeking this rush of feelings of my flesh that would make me forget the wrongs, that would give me this *Mary Poppins* glee, and a heart full of love for them.

None of that happened, but what did happen was a slow and steady change by releasing the resentment, the anger, the need to punish them, the need to vindicate their wrongs against me. I don't know where I heard this but unforgiveness is like drinking poison and expecting the other person to die, when in fact you are just poisoning your own life. I believe God calls us to forgive for our own well-being so we can trust Him with the outcome.

Forgiveness is not condoning the egregious actions, but letting God fight my battles. God's word is also clear that as we forgive, we are forgiven.

> *"But if you do not forgive others their sins, your Father will not forgive your sins" (Matthew 6:15).*

You can't get much clearer than that. Forgiveness is not an act that can be done in our own strength. Forgiveness is a process that we sometimes must undergo again and again. Forgiveness can only be done by the power of the Holy Spirit.

In my weakness, I cry out, "Jesus, help me to forgive," over and over, seventy times seven.

> *"Then came Peter to him, and said, Lord, how oft shall my brother sin against me, and I forgive him? Till seven times? Jesus said to him, I say not to you, Until seven times: but, Until seventy times seven"* *(Matthew 18:21–22).*

Why forgive? Why release the wrongs? Why release the person? Forgiveness brings us peace. Our peace is so critical to happiness, to our ability to thrive. Some people are just filled with evil who want to rob our peace. We often want to think the best of everyone, myself included. God tells us not to count that spirit as anything until you test it. You test it by prayer and time. Time always tells. Time always reveals, and time always resolves. Even those who are filled with evil can have an encounter with God and be saved. I believe in my heart of hearts that God calls us all to Himself—some will receive, and some will reject.

> *"Dear friends, do not believe every spirit, but test the spirits to see whether they are from God, because many false prophets have gone out into the world. This is how you can recognize the Spirit of God: Every spirit that acknowledges that Jesus Christ has come in the flesh is from God, but every spirit that does not acknowledge Jesus is not from God. This is the spirit of the antichrist, which you have heard is coming and even now is already in the world. You, dear children, are from God and have overcome them, because the one who is in you is greater than the one who is in the world"* (1 John 4: 1–4).

You can end friendships that are no longer healthy or positive. It may be hard, and it may hurt. We often try too hard, but I've realized it's okay to grow apart from people because your lives, your seasons, your beliefs have changed. Not all relationships are meant to last forever. Remember people are in our lives for a reason, a season, or a lifetime.

I am careful with my time. Pay attention to

who you invest your time and energy into. It's good and healthy to be intentional about who you invest your time and talents in. Your time is limited, and a precious gift, and your friendship even more valuable.

Relationships can either pull you up or drag you down. When you step out of your comfort zone and pursue others, you're offering them something precious: your heart and your time. Family bonds or friendships don't survive without investing time and energy and grace. Spending time together, being authentic, real, and vulnerable, is where true relationships flourish. I try to surround myself with those who lift me higher and try hard to not take them for granted.

Relationships are one of life's greatest treasures, especially the most intimate ones. I've learned in my marriage to try to give what I need. If I need a hug, I give a hug. If I need time, I give time. If I need an ear, I give an ear. Sometimes when we give, we get filled up. Loving others well is a part of loving me.

CHAPTER 5

Love Perpetuates

"The LORD appeared to us in the past, saying: "I have loved you with an everlasting love; I have drawn you with unfailing kindness. I will build you up again, and you, Virgin Israel, will be rebuilt. Again you will take up your timbrels and go out to dance with the joyful" (Jeremiah 33:3–4).

There are many toxic emotions that try to creep into our minds and attack our peace, as a residual of abuse — unforgiveness, resentment, hatred, bitterness, disappointment, anger, guilt, shame, sadness, self-defeating. These toxic emotions, unchecked, can eat us alive. It's not that we won't experience these emotions from time to time, but when these emotions consume our thought-life and siphon energy, they become toxic.

These constant thoughts are deadly and can open the door to evil and create strongholds in our lives. The battle of the mind is fought moment by moment, battle by battle. Combating evil is the most constant and fierce battle waged in your life. You see, I believe that we don't truly acknowledge what John 10:10 says, that Satan comes to *"KILL, STEAL, and DESTROY."* Well, spiritual things are much more important than material things. So guess what? He *has* come to *"KILL, STEAL, and DESTROY."* It's our life, mental health, our relationship(s), our health, our hearts, passions, joy, peace, and good will. We must be on guard at all times.

> *"For our struggle is not against flesh and blood, but against the rulers, against the authorities, against the powers of this dark world and against the spiritual forces of evil in the heavenly realms" (Ephesians 6:12).*

The most powerful weapon we have to fight evil is our faith, covering, and perpetual love of Jesus Christ. I believe all those who call on the name of Jesus will be saved and immediately have the power to overcome evil with good. So many heartbroken and abused have walked through life barren of hope and happiness. It is my prayer that this cycle ends.

As in my life, and the many I have ministered to, I've observed the unresolved trauma of abuse as it festers and manifests into a life of bitterness, resentment, hate, addiction, self-defeating behaviors, codependence, PTSD, and a long list of trauma-related mental illnesses. It doesn't have to continue. I found victory and healing, and so can you.

We have the ability, and it begins with our faith in Jesus Christ and the perpetual love He abundantly pours out to us. We have to wake up to the trauma-related issues that cause our suffering and acknowledge that downward emotional spirals are rooted in the abuse. We have to also acknowledge that these issues are all weapons Satan uses against us in spiritual warfare, and we must learn how to respond and defend against these attacks.

Many people, even those in "the church,"

don't acknowledge the evil power of Satan. Jesus has already conquered evil, so He is our greatest source of strength and our refuge. There is no other way to defend against the schemes of Satan without Jesus Christ as Lord of your life. It's a simple decision, one that will change your life for eternity.

If you have never asked Jesus Christ into your heart, there is no better time than this very moment. It's as simple as a commitment, a prayer, and faith to believe. When you say "yes" to welcoming Jesus into your heart, you possess the greatest love force the world has ever known.

> *"For God so loved the world that He gave His only begotten Son, that whoever believes in Him should not perish but have everlasting life. For God did not send His Son into the world to condemn the world, but that the world through Him might be saved" (John 3:16–17).*

Inviting Jesus Christ into your heart as Lord of your life is as easy as saying and truly meaning the words in this prayer:

> *Dear Lord Jesus, I know that I am a sinner, and I ask Your forgiveness. I believe You*

are the son of God, came to earth as flesh,
died on the cross as a sacrifice for my sins,
and rose on the third day from the dead, so
that I can be united with God the Father. I
turn from my sins and invite You to come
into my heart and life. I want to trust and
follow You as my Savior and my Lord. In
Jesus's name, amen.

I accepted Jesus when I was twelve, and I truly believe Jesus gave me the strength to endure the abuse until my escape. I rededicated my life and was baptized as a young woman and have lived a life of faith and know whatever I face in this life, I do not face it alone.

"The Lord himself goes before you and will be
with you; he will never leave you nor forsake
you. Do not be afraid; do not be discouraged"
(Deuteronomy 31:8).

Your salvation decision is the greatest decision of your life. This decision is a commitment to live for Jesus Christ. If you have taken this step of faith, I pray you will notify me so I can pray for you and encourage you.

There have been many people who have helped me along my healing journey, both inside and outside the church. Their perpetual love and acceptance has taught me how to love myself more. Connecting to a church home can be intimidating, especially if you were not raised in a church, experienced judgment from a Christian, or you have no experience of a faith family.

I pray you take the step to seek a church fellowship, close to your home. Perhaps you have a friend who is involved in a church you can visit so you will not be alone. Please be mindful that people are flawed, and don't expect perfection. You may need to visit several different churches and pray that God leads you to where He wants you to learn, grow in your faith, and serve.

My healing has also included professional counseling, and if I become overwhelmed, I still seek help. Seeking professional help from a medical or mental health professional is not a sign of weakness, but strength. Healing is closer than you think, but too many are blinded when help is in plain sight. If we don't seek help, we tend to march around the same mountain of turmoil, continue on the same merry-go-round, and it can be exhausting. When we keep walking toward the darkness, our world becomes very dark and bleak. When we walk toward the light, slowly but surely, our lives become brighter.

> *"It is shameful even to mention what the disobedient do in secret. But everything exposed by the light becomes visible – and everything that is illuminated becomes a light. This is why it is said:*
>   *'Wake up, sleeper,*
>   *rise from the dead,*
>   *and Christ will shine on you'"* (Ephesians 5:12–14).

The darkness opens the door for evil to enter our lives. The world today consumes so much of our focus and attention that we feel like there is never enough time, resources, space, or support to truly heal from the heinous acts inflicted upon us. We have to be intentional and give ourselves time and space to heal. Even trying to process grief over the loss of a loved one is often rushed in our hectic world.

I think there is so much abuse in our society that our world has become oblivious to it. It's as if society has accepted abuse as the norm, and we shall never speak of it. Weak and wounded, we keep moving in life, with the dark cloud of abuse shadowing us, perhaps we act out in horrific ways and fall into the next abusive relationship, thus continuing the cycle.

I believe our mental health system is incapable

of meeting the needs of those with trauma. We have a mental health crisis. We need to make mental health more accessible, more affordable, and more accepted. A healthy mind is just as important as a healthy body.

I was in a Georgia House of Representatives hearing some years ago where it was disclosed that 179 counties in Georgia, my home state, with a population of 10.3 million had only 329 licensed mental health professionals. At the time, this meant that there was only one mental health professional for every 31,306 people in Georgia. That statistic just floored me. Does that seem acceptable? No, absolutely not. Mental Health America's "Access to Care Ranking 2023" report puts Georgia forty-ninth out of fifty-one states, including DC.[2]

This huge social crisis is playing out in lives lost to the dark evil forces of this world. Random shootings in small towns, schools, and churches happen frequently. Human trafficking is at an all-time high. Children abused in their homes is rampant.

People who are struggling emotionally want and need acceptance. So much so that they are

---

[2] https://mhanational.org/issues/2023/mental-health-america-access-care-data.

prone to being lured into evil actions, gangs, cults, or any group that may wish to control their thoughts and actions.

Our very social foundation is being rocked. We are surrounded by and have been desensitized to so much evil to the point where we've become indifferent to it. Some may say that, culturally, we have an infatuation with the occult. Our media feeds us a steady appetite of vampires, witches, and satanic content that is threatening our culture's moral underpinnings.

> *"When you enter the land the Lord your God is giving you, do not learn to imitate the detestable ways of the nations there. Let no one be found among you who sacrifices their son or daughter in the fire, who practices divination or sorcery, interprets omens, engages in witchcraft, or casts spells, or who is a medium or spiritist or who consults the dead" (Deuteronomy 18:9–11).*

Hollywood has entertained us with witchcraft, vampires, and occult-themed content, which have subtly introduced and inserted topics into our social thought and acceptance. My generation watched *Bewitched*, one of *TV Guide*'s "Top 50 Rated Shows of All Time." We watch it, we laugh, and didn't think a whole lot about it, but it was bringing it right into our living rooms in a lighthearted way.

Stop and think about how much TV has fed us violence, vampires, witches, aliens, the occult. It's a lot.

> *"But the cowardly, the unbelieving, the vile, the murderers, the sexually immoral, those who practice magic arts, the idolaters and all liars — they will be consigned to the fiery lake of burning sulfur. This is the second death" (Revelation 21:8).*

I am addressing this topic because of the spiritual battle that is ongoing. Satan wants to keep you locked up and weighed down with the garbage of shame, guilt, remorse, unforgiveness, anger. He knows that Jesus has already provided your healing and redeemed you through His death on the cross—but Satan doesn't want you to know it, and he certainly doesn't want you to walk in the power and authority of a child of God. These dark shows and evil content are ways to keep up the attack, and it grieves God. God wants you to have freedom, and Satan will do whatever he can to keep hooks in us even if it is being entertained by a movie that glorifies evil.

"You, my brothers and sisters, were called to be free. But do not use your freedom to indulge the flesh; rather, serve one another humbly in love. For the entire law is fulfilled in keeping this one command: 'Love your neighbor as yourself.' If you bite and devour each other, watch out or you will be destroyed by each other.

"So I say, walk by the Spirit, and you will not gratify the desires of the flesh. "For the flesh desires what is contrary to the Spirit, and the Spirit what is contrary to the flesh. They are in conflict with each other, so that you are not to do whatever you want. "But if you are led by the Spirit, you are not under the law.

"The acts of the flesh are obvious: sexual immorality, impurity and debauchery; idolatry and witchcraft; hatred, discord, jealousy, fits of rage, selfish ambition, dissensions, factions and envy; drunkenness, orgies, and the like. I warn you, as I did before, that those who live like this will not inherit the kingdom of God.

"But the fruit of the Spirit is love, joy, peace, forbearance, kindness, goodness, faithfulness, gentleness and self-control. Against such things there is no law. Those

who belong to Christ Jesus have crucified the flesh with its passions and desires. Since we live by the Spirit, let us keep in step with the Spirit. Let us not become conceited, provoking and envying each other" (Galatians 5:13–26).

I know that it's a long verse but it's so powerful. The first words, "We were called to be free" — I want the perpetual love force that sets me free and is the sword and shield that fights the evil force that comes to "KILL, STEAL, and DESTROY." I believe that love force to be Jesus Christ, the son of God, who is seated at the right hand of God, interceding on my behalf and your behalf. Take refuge in God, and trust God can do what He said He can do.

The question is, how can you be saved from this evil world? The only answer is to surrender your life to Jesus Christ. When good and evil clash, there is a battle at hand. A battle against good and evil, right and wrong, peace and war — a battle against silence and freedom, a battle against your dreams and your unbelief, a battle against hurting and healing — a battle that you can only win with Christ.

"And he said, 'What comes out of a person

*is what defiles him. For from within, out of
the heart of man, come evil thoughts, sexual
immorality, theft, murder, adultery,
coveting, wickedness, deceit, sensuality,
envy, slander, pride, foolishness. All these
evil things come from within, and they
defile a person'"* (Mark 7:20–23).

In our abuse, we were defiled by a force of evil.
The abuse convinced us to believe lies. Your lie
may be different than my lie, but the thread is the
curse of shame, the cruel words that pierced our
souls. Our bodies hold the memories of the pain
of the emotional and physical attacks. Memories
are tormenting, and we scream if not audibly,
silently as vivid and repressed memories visit us.
They come in the night in nightmares; they come
in the day with triggers. It may be a smell, a
sound, or a touch that triggers the thought of the
abusive event. In these moments we relive the
attack all over again, feel the sensations, the fear,
the shame.

In my thirties, I was diagnosed with post-
traumatic stress disorder (PTSD), which is a
mental health disorder in which we have
difficulty recovering after experiencing or
witnessing a traumatic event. The condition may
last months or years, with triggers that can bring

back memories of the trauma accompanied by intense emotional and physical reactions. I suffered severely in my twenties and thirties, but in the last fifteen years or so, events have been few and far between.

Symptoms may include nightmares or unwanted memories of the trauma, avoidance of situations that bring back memories of the trauma, heightened reactions, anxiety, or depressed mood. I've experienced panic attacks as part of my PTSD. I've been triggered in such a way that my body couldn't cope with the pain of the memory. I know there are a lot of psychological definitions for PTSD, but for me, I become so overwhelmed with pain of the present and real memory that I can't breathe, I can't think, I can't control my muscular movement, I can't get grounded in the now and present. I'm sure others could describe it more eloquently, but when I have a panic attack it takes me back steps in my healing.

I am truly blessed to not have had (knock on wood) a panic attack in a few years, but I'm sad to say my daughter witnessed the last attack. I've been blessed to have been able to hide them over the years. My sweet husband has experienced several, but most I have had alone. I am so grateful every time to arrive on the other side, panting for long minutes to catch my breath, to ground myself, to come back to reality, finding the here and now, where I am not in that memory, that place in time that terrified me and made me someone else.

Friends, the healing journey is a long and arduous one that we must commit to stay the course. We have to be kind to ourselves on this journey, because we can feel as though we can clap our hands and be healed. I wish it were that easy, but there will be unpredictable occasions where our trauma creeps in and we have to deal with the moment in a healthy way, not beating ourselves up or throwing in the towel, negating the healing progress.

To my daughter who will read this one day, I say thank you and I am so sorry you had to experience my meltdown(s). She cared for me in such a compassionate and clinical way, never judging, just compassionate care and concern. She had me slow down my breathing and focus on an object in the room. She had me ground my thoughts to the present. Within a few minutes, I was back and the panic attack had subsided but not my extreme embarrassment for putting my family through such an ordeal.

I was so determined to not let dysfunction

creep into my family. But, I confess, no matter how hard I tried, my childhood dysfunction crept into our lives. I am happy to report, it did not destroy our lives, but it definitely left its fingerprints. After my last panic attack, I did not beat myself up. I realized that this is just part of the healing journey, as it was not as severe as past attacks. I must press into my healing and be good to myself.

The most effective practice that helped me through these events is grounding in the present. "Grounding" literally means connecting to the ground, but the term is also used to describe a way to bring one's traumatic and anxious thoughts back to the present to ground yourself mentally. Grounding reduces stress by decreasing our levels of cortisol, commonly known as the stress hormone. The release of too much cortisol in your body from long-term stress can cause the adrenal glands to become overworked and can lead to physical health problems.

The following are some grounding techniques that have been successful for me in helping my brain manage overwhelming thoughts and feelings.

1. **Meditate on scripture.** I have memorized verses of scripture that help ground

me in truth. Repeating these verses along with prayer helps give me strength for the painful moments to pass. God's word is power; God's word is healing. There are so many promises of God. Sometimes, I just search the internet for the promises of God and that is a great place for me to learn how much I am loved.

There is a great story in the New Testament of scripture where a woman had been hurting, bleeding for twelve years, and she reached for Jesus to touch the hem of His garment and was instantly healed. I feel like the more I reach for Jesus, the more I am healed.

"So Jesus got up and went with him, along with His disciples. Suddenly a woman who had suffered from bleeding for twelve years came up behind Him and touched the fringe of His cloak. She said to herself, "If only I touch His cloak, I will be healed." Jesus turned and saw her. "Take courage, daughter," He said, "your faith has healed you." And the woman was cured from that very hour" (Matthew 9:19–22).

2. **Stay in the present moment.** Our mind tends to want to take us back in time, and memories can feel very real. Meditation teaches us to focus on our breath and turn our attention to the present. This is known as mindfulness. Try not to let your mind wander to thoughts of negativity, fear, or all the "what ifs" that cause us to spiral into a panic. Take in everything happening right now and take some deep breaths from your abdomen. I practice breathing in for five seconds and out for ten seconds until I regain my composure. Fear has a way of overwhelming us. I suggest audibly telling yourself, "I am safe in this present moment, and the attacks of the past are in the past."

3. **Touch or hold something from the earth.** Pick up a rock or touch a leaf on a tree. Rub your hand over a tree's bark. Notice the details of what you are touching — the little imperfections, grooves, notches, etc. What does it feel like? Is it rough or smooth? Warm or cold?

Every living thing has its own energy,

so handling these natural items certainly counts as practicing grounding! Water and fire ground me like nothing else. I like to be close to large bodies of water—a lake, the ocean, or even a swimming pool. My favorite thing to do is dig my feet into the hot sand on the seashore or the green grass outside. Lighting a fire in the fireplace or just watching the wick of a candle burn seem to take me to a peaceful place. When memories torment me, finding peace is my goal.

4. **Step out of your comfort zone.** Breaking a routine and getting away from the familiar can cause its own kind of anxiety. Venturing into the unknown can be scary, but it can also be extremely healthy. Think of it as rising to a new challenge. Trying something new and getting out of a mental "rut" forces you to shift your focus and energy to a new activity. Whether it's agreeing to a hike, 5K walk/run, or volunteering for a cause you care about, it's good to set a goal or do something kind for yourself or others to take your mind off your own worries.

5. **Pay attention to your senses.** Tune into your senses the next time you're outside and/or practicing grounding and experience the sights, smells, tastes, and sounds. Keep your eyes open to take in the view around you. Now close them and shift to your other senses. What does it smell like? Do you smell fresh cut grass, the crisp running water from a stream, or the unique scent of flowers or trees? Tune into the sounds. Do you hear birds, the rustle of leaves, the rush of water? How about taste? Do your taste buds respond differently to being outside? I try to capture these moments in my mind so when I am restless and can't sleep or am fearful, I quiet my mind and replay these sensory pleasures.

6. **Listen to soft music.** My personal love is piano music, but if I am feeling unsettled or just want to clear my mind, listening to instrumental music helps to relax me. My favorite is Stanton Lanier. He is a very talented and anointed pianist.

Self-care is critical to loving me. Loving yourself gives you the force to recognize and battle t evil in your life. I welcome all that is good in my life. Good does overcome evil. We must receive the perpetual love of God and rest in that love so we will be healed and set free from the bondage of abuse.

CHAPTER 6

A Lifetime of Love

"He remembered us in our low estate His love endures forever. and freed us from our enemies. His love endures forever. He gives food to every creature. His love endures forever. Give thanks to the God of heaven. His love endures forever" (Psalm 136: 23–26).

We have but one life to live. Time is so precious and fleeting. Every year seems to go by faster and faster. I cannot begin to describe how much I love to travel. I quiver with anticipation when I plan a trip, *especially* if it is a new destination I've never been. This is how I approach my lifetime of healing. I want to be the healthiest person I can be for me, for you and for all those I love. I want to live life with great expectation and anticipation for every day, and the treasure it holds. I want love to fill my life for a lifetime and be intentional about removing the obstacles to this lifetime of love.

Taking a personal inventory of those obstacles is difficult. It takes an internal introspection of things in your life you can recognize and control, to perpetuate this lifetime of love in your life. That inventory should focus on your priorities. We have such a short time on this earth—even if we live to be one hundred.

I'm in my late fifties and it seems like a blip on the radar. This life is full of ebb and flow, from sadness to joy, disappointment to triumph. So, in this inventory, I must prioritize the important fundamentals in this lifetime of love. My priorities are those with a lasting legacy, which I believe is most prevalent in the lives we touch.

To love God with all my heart, mind, and soul is my number one priority, by worship and obedience to His way and will. Through my close relationship with God, I have an anointing of His peace and presence. And I long to share that peace and presence.

My second priority is my precious husband and soul mate, Phil, and fostering a healthy, loving, and sound marriage. I must admit he doesn't always get top priority, but I truly try. I feel successful in having a clean, warm, inviting home that is our sanctuary. I try to be home almost every evening so we can unwind and enjoy dinner and precious time together.

Though we get engrossed in our own interests, just knowing he is close, holding his hand, or knowing all is well with the world because I see him brings me so much comfort. I wish I could bottle that happiness, and I want to protect it with all my heart. I'm so blessed because he is such a simple man with few demands.

He is willing to be the hero of any "honey-do" list. His encouragement makes me think I can move any mountain. It is an amazing feeling to have someone believe in you more than you believe in yourself. He also holds me accountable and has an unwavering, strong faith in God that inspires me. He is my world, and I am grateful God sent me a soul mate to journey through life hand in hand. His love fills me up to overflowing. Having Phil by my side and experiencing his love as a constant in my life has expedited my healing and helped me to love myself.

My children, though grown, still need me in some capacity — or at least, I believe so — although those needs are more difficult to decipher than ever before. If you are a parent of adults, you can probably relate. I want to be there for them, but I don't want to intrude. I want to share wisdom without them interpreting that I am telling them what to do. I want to be there, but I don't want to rob them of time with their spouse or children.

I feel as though my children had to live through some of my difficult days of healing, and for that I feel they were robbed of some of their innocence. I also believe they may have learned something from a very early age that imprinted on their destiny.

Through my healing journey and ministry work, they were exposed to the toxic topic of child sexual abuse. I did not realize the secondhand trauma they experienced until years later. I am blessed to have stopped the cycle of abuse in my family. I want nothing more than to continue to love my children and my grandchildren and be present. I want to be truly invested in their lives, always present for them for a lifetime.

A healthy family can be a great emotional support, in good times and bad. These are the sweetest relationships I will ever experience.

As for my extended family, I try to be the glue. I try to keep everyone engaged, but it's hard. Everyone seems to be busy and have their own lives, but I keep trying. I remember my granny was so invested in the family unit. She was the nucleus of our family, hosting lunch most Sundays. With families living farther and farther apart, it is also challenging to have quality time together, and technology has made it so impersonal.

I want to continue my granny's legacy, as she gave so much of herself to her family. The first time I made homemade biscuits, cakes, casseroles, I realized how much of a labor of love and a time-consuming task she put forth every Sunday. She rarely took a shortcut and always had a spread on the dinner table. In her retirement, when she barely had the means to care for herself, she never stopped giving, because she knew God would always provide. That is strong faith, selfless love, and a beautiful legacy.

I am so blessed with precious friendships throughout my life. I have a close-knit, small core group that I've had for twenty-plus years. It has evolved as some have moved or passed away. I love lasting relationships with history and shared experiences. It seems as you grow, as you show up for them, they show up for you with our ups and downs, disappointments and joys, wins and losses. This enriches my lifetime of love.

I want to invest in a lifetime of loving others through ministry. Angela's Voice, together with partners, will be a *voice* to and for the hurting. No one deserves to be abused, and we must join together to better prevent and protect others from abuse, especially children.

How do I love me in a way that gives these relationships what they need to flourish? I believe a way to foster these relationships is with grace, engagement, time, and presence.

Personally, I have identified my stumbling blocks and try to avoid them at all costs. I have learned that I don't have to be right all the time, and I'd rather be happy than right. I am learning to have better self-control. I am learning to listen and think before I speak, to guard the words that come out of my mouth, ensuring they build people up instead of tear them down.

> *"'As for me, this is my covenant with them,' says the Lord. 'My Spirit, who is on you, will not depart from you, and my words that I have put in your mouth will always be on your lips, on the lips of your children and on the lips of their descendants — from this time on and forever,' says the Lord"* (Isaiah 59:21).

I try to minimize the potential for drama in my life. Those of us who are struggling with past trauma may allow that trauma to bleed into the lives of those we love. We may act out as a result of past hurts. If we are a member of a dysfunctional family, we may be drawn into their difficult situations. Sometimes, in trying to stay connected to a dysfunctional family, an endless cycle of drama is part of the norm. Drama is exhausting and emotionally damaging. I have prayed those generational curses off of my family and my generation forward. We must be intentional about protecting ourselves against dysfunction.

Only Jesus Christ and His love can heal our families, can fill that hole in our hearts left by neglect, abandonment, and abuse. The aftermath of abuse is a chapter of my life I would love to forget. Fortunately, I am surrounded with supportive, forgiving, loving family and friends. But, of course, there are always some people, as you may also experience, who have no compassion for your trauma. We have to understand they lack the compassion gene. Either we can choose to have them in our lives, realizing they are not our go-to person, or we need or eliminate them from our lives.

Guess what? It's our choice. I am not interested in investing in relationships that are superficial. We can find plenty of those on social media. I desire to invest in relationships that are deep and meaningful.

I am also not interested in competing with anyone but want to celebrate others' successes. I did not always behave this way. I spent many years playing the comparison game and feeling like I never measured up. I had an envious spirit that was a generational curse I had to break off my life. I looked around and saw it everywhere in my family; it was toxic. I saw it play out and it was downright poisonous. So, I had to take power over that toxic emotion, know my journey is different, and bless those God chooses to bless and help those that are struggling with a hand up.

We live in an environment of division, anger, and confusion. It is up to us to understand the devastation of abuse and educate others. Childhood sexual abuse murders innocence and puts a heavy burden on the abused to recover. Domestic violence creates such confusion over the definition of love, as it is so distorted and manipulated by the perpetrator.

This lifetime of love means, again and again, striving to be a better person, falling down and getting back up, failing and forgiving yourself and others. You have but one lifetime and when your days are done, I wish nothing more than for you to be memorialized for loving well in this lifetime.

CHAPTER 7

Love Heals

*"Nevertheless, I will bring health and **healing** to it; I will heal my people and will let them enjoy abundant peace and security"* (Jeremiah 33:6).

I could never as eloquently describe present healing as my dear friend Theresa Harvard Johnson. She shares that we spend so much of our time looking for healing and seeking people to help us heal. According to Theresa, our journey is both spiritual and natural. We are healed in the natural with help from others, then we are healing in the spiritual by the power of Jesus Christ. She goes on to explain that we are not only "healing out of a situation" but "healing into the MIND of Christ," which elevates us spiritually through a closer relationship with Jesus. When you experience His presence, you long for that intimacy. That spiritual elevation is a result of healing.

When healing comes, it's not just our natural situation that changes but there is a "spiritual elevation," or a shift, that must occur to keep us there in our mind.

> *"For to set the mind on the flesh is death, but to set the mind on the spirit is life and peace"* (Romans 8:6).

Could it be that we strive to heal for our own situational relief and it has hindered us? Are we limiting the testimony of our healing to Christ's works, miracles, and signs? Or are we charged with not only having our circumstances resolved but also becoming like Christ in the consideration of our situations and suffering? Is the end game just healing from the problem so we can go on, or is there an *inward transformation* within the mind of Christ that we *must* apprehend? The latter is a living *from* the mind of Christ that we have been given. We are to daily grow into *His mind* through our circumstances and suffering.

Without acknowledging this part of the healing process, we might linger too long on self. We might receive partial healing or momentary relief without ever obtaining the prize of ascension.

All healing for us as believers is an act of reconciliation. All healing for us as believers is an intricate part of Christ's filling of all things. It's not just our pain that He heals but the framework around our perception of it. It's not just our preoccupation with sins that He deals with but our ability to address the mind-sets that guide it. We are not *only* healed of our earthbound concerns internally but we are healed into *greater fullness* — the kind of fullness that is not predicated on whether our circumstances change because they may not. We rely on ascending into the kind of healing that defined Jesus's entire life: the grace of God really is sufficient.

Having the mind of Christ is to be filled with peace, joy, and love. I love being happy. I love to smile. Now I realize being happy 24/7 is not 100 percent possible but coming close sure feels good.

I remember many years ago, I was in a convertible (Phil and I were on a trip driving down the Pacific Coast Highway, and we booked a convertible sports car) but ended up with a compact black-top, teal convertible. This was our convertible chariot of choice from the rental car company, as it was the only one available. We were booked in quaint bed-and-breakfasts, roaming from winery to winery, beach to beach — living the dream.

I remember feeling so very happy in one moment and terrified something awful was going to happen the next. I remember almost the moment I heard very clearly, "the other shoe is not going to drop." In other words, stop anticipating something horrible will happen and enjoy the moment, the here and now. It was a moment in time that I peeled off the spirit of fear and oppression. I can't say it was a 180-degree turnaround but it was a shift in my course. Guess what happens when you shift the longitude and latitude of a waypoint on a ship? You head for a totally different destination. My destination of choice: happy.

Happiness is not a place; it's a state of mind, it's a determined will. You will never follow the exact same path tomorrow as you did today. We get one chance every minute to choose happiness, to choose to protect our peace, to choose our battles, to choose whether it is more important to be right or be happy, to say no, to guard our boundaries.

All moment-by-moment choices because every decision leads to our destiny.

> *"A happy heart makes the face cheerful, but heartache crushes the spirit" (Proverbs 15:13).*

> *"I know that there is nothing better for people than to be happy and to do good while they live" (Ecclesiastes 3:12).*

> *"Moreover, when God gives someone wealth and possessions, and the ability to enjoy them, to accept their lot and be happy in their toil – this is a gift of God" (Ecclesiastes 5:19).*

God desires us to be happy. I'll take it one step further and say that God wants us healed so we can have abundant joy in our lives. The prophet Isaiah says it so well:

> *"The Spirit of the Sovereign Lord is on me, because the Lord has anointed me to proclaim good news to the poor. He has sent me to bind up the brokenhearted, to proclaim freedom for the captives and release from darkness for the prisoners, to*

proclaim the year of the Lord's favor and the day of vengeance of our God, to comfort all who mourn, and provide for those who grieve in Zion — to bestow on them a crown of beauty instead of ashes, the oil of joy instead of mourning, and a garment of praise instead of a spirit of despair. They will be called oaks of righteousness, a planting of the Lord for the display of his splendor" (Isaiah 61:1–3).

There are always those who just don't want to see you happy. If you are prospering spiritually, emotionally, relationally, and/or financially, there are people who just want to see you fail. There is a comparative, competitive, envious, judgmental "yuckiness" that filters their perception and engagement with you. Shed those folks in your life — run.

My dear friend Deborah always tells me, *"Everyone is not meant to be on your journey. Just do you, boo, because everyone else is taken."* Surround yourself with cheerleaders, those who want you to get to the next rung on the ladder. And guess what? They've already got their hands interlaced under your foot to boost you to the next rung on the ladder of life, especially when you don't have the strength to take the step yourself. I have been extremely blessed to have those friendships in my life. When I was at the bottom, more than once, I had a friend to pull me to the surface.

Julie was one of my cheerleaders and lifesavers. She was my best friend in high school and the only person I had confided the abuse I was suffering in my homelife. I remember so vividly when Julie (God rest her soul, she passed in her teens) was the one I ran to in the middle of the night at the lowest moment of my life. That night, I had attempted suicide multiple times and was a mess. The next morning her family opened the door to their home, stood in the gap for me, and assured me of my freedom from the chaos I had endured for so long. She drove me back to my parents the next day to collect my meek belongings.

I never thought my mother would desert me. I never thought she would stand with my abuser, knowing all he had done to me. When I arrived, my mom handed me a hefty trash bag as my sisters were crying and begging me not to go. I remember looking back as we drove down the driveway, knowing I would never be touched by him again. It was a mix of emotions — fear, relief, freedom, and hope. Hope that, somehow, I could begin to live, shed the fear, and look toward the future with optimism.

My other precious friend Deborah is my prayer warrior. She will phone me regularly and share all God has revealed to her and pray with me. Her call and prayers never fail to relate to the struggles I am dealing with at that moment. She builds me up, pushes me to the next level, keeps my faith focused and keen, and sharpens me (iron sharpens iron). Everyone needs to have a friend in their life like Deborah for encouragement and accountability, who speaks truth, whether I want to hear it or not. I do not know what I would do without Deborah, my prayer warrior in the spiritual realm and a powerful minister of truth.

And then there is my precious Jaye who has such a tender heart. It blesses me so much because she loves intentionally. She is the best cheerleader for her inner circle. Jaye worked tirelessly alongside me in ministering to survivors. Jaye is a movie director and so incredibly talented. She used those talents to create amazing public service announcements to build awareness around the issues of child sexual abuse. Now she is directing impactful films that speak to the heart of life's journey. Her work is inspiring, healing, and thought provoking.

It is a joy to have family and friends praying for your dreams while you are cheering on their dreams. In my opinion, we should celebrate with each other more. We should celebrate our different sizes, opinions, tastes, dreams, and lives. The love from above, from our Heavenly Father, and the immense love that surrounds us through beautiful relationships, helps us to heal, and through that love, we can love ourselves more.

As these relationships bring out the best in us, we are able to give the best of ourselves to others. I encourage you to look around and nurture those relationships you cherish and shed those that are unhealthy. This type of love from above and from around heals us, providing a constant source of encouragement, comfort, and strength.

CHAPTER 8

Love Within

*"Create in me a pure heart, O God, and renew a steadfast spirit **within** me"* *(Psalm 51:10).*

You are uniquely you. God created only one of you and every fiber of your being is unique. God is in you, in every cell of your being. Laminin is the protein network foundation for providing instruction to cells and the formation of organs. The laminins are an important and biologically active part of the basal lamina, influencing cell differentiation, migration, and adhesion. Laminin is vital to the survival and formation of tissues. It is no accident that laminin is in the shape of a cross. I've often questioned how God could know me as I was being formed in my mother's womb or know me so intimately that He even knows the number of hairs on my head. Well, this could be the answer. Celebrate your uniqueness and your identity to be the greatest version of you possible.

Your story is a combination of your beliefs. Your belief controls your identity. Your beliefs about your abuse can create and they can destroy. My prayer is that they will create in you a desire to heal and love yourself today as God loves you.

If you believe with absolute certainty that you can have an amazing life, you will. Life is a battle, but your words are powerful in winning that battle. Words impact your biochemistry and your beliefs. I encourage you to think about how you define your life. If you think life is a test—where you are being judged—it's stressful, it's pass or fail. But if you believe life is sacred, it is special, precious, and peaceful.

What if you define life as a gift? Well, then it's treasured, a surprise. What if you define life as a dance? Then you think of words like playful, expressive, joyous, and constant movement. Life is whatever you decide it is in your mind. We must be conscious of how we define life, conscious of our belief system, and know we have the power to change it.

Lasting change always requires a change in our identity. I no longer wanted to be the victim, living insecure and afraid. So, I changed my identity to be a victor living the life I chose. Our identity is the most powerful force in the human personality. We possess a strong need to stay consistent with how we define ourselves. When we change our identity, we change our behavior, how we think, feel, what we are willing to do to accomplish our dreams. Some of us created our identity based on outside forces twenty, thirty, or forty years ago. There is more to you than what has happened to you. You are not who you have been; you are who you are becoming.

Your mind is a great tool to redefine your identity and who you want to be. Ask yourself, *What does my identity need to be to have the quality of life I want?* You have a choice today to have an extraordinary life, to enjoy more, experience more, and be more than you ever dreamed. Stretch yourself. If you believe you can't, then you *must*. That's called breakthrough. The secret is momentum, because one success catapults you to the next success. Just say yes to your dreams and watch them manifest. YES, YES, YES!

The most powerful force of change is our focus, mentally and physically. When we put our mind and bodies in a peak state with lots of energy, we can make a shift in our identity by feeding our minds with all that is pure and positive.

What is a peak state? A peak state is the condition of our body. What does our face say? Are we breathing shallow or deep, standing strong or hunching over? Be conscious of your body movement and expressions. If you want to change how you feel, change your body chemistry. When we change our physical state, our focus, and our language, we change how we feel. Words create meaning, so choose your words carefully. If you say, "I am depressed," you are more likely to identify as being a depressed person, but if you say, "I am struggling with depression *today*," you are not attaching depression to your identity. Words create emotion and reality.

> *"Rejoice in the Lord always. I will say it again: Rejoice! Let your gentleness be evident to all. The Lord is near. Do not be anxious about anything, but in every situation, by prayer and petition, with thanksgiving, present your requests to God. And the peace of God, which*

transcends all understanding, will guard your hearts and your minds in Christ Jesus.

"Finally, brothers and sisters, whatever is true, whatever is noble, whatever is right, whatever is pure, whatever is lovely, whatever is admirable — if anything is excellent or praiseworthy — think about such things. Whatever you have learned or received or heard from me, or seen in me — put it into practice. And the God of peace will be with you" (Philippians 4:4–8).

I have learned to create incantations for my identity that I routinely repeat which complete the sentence "I am . . ."

- *"I am good."*
- *"I am strong."*
- *"I am courageous."*
- *"I am loved."*
- *"I am at peace."*
- *"I am cherished."*

Anything you add to the end of "I am . . ." you become. I encourage you to create a clear list of who you are to help create your compelling future. Choice is an unbelievable gift. We can choose how we react, how we feel, what we focus on, what we tell ourselves, what meaning we give to pain.

In my struggle to love myself, I defined my identity and made a list of my characteristics that I loved. This was a way for me to recognize and start to appreciate those characteristics, like other people appreciated those characteristics. I took inventory so I could accept the truth of who I really was in God's eyes and in friends' eyes and not who I had been led to believe I was through my abuser's eyes.

I love Jesus.

I love Jesus with all my heart, mind, and soul and do my very best to love my neighbor as myself. That is the greatest commandment. Though I am not a Bible scholar, I love God's word. I am in God's word consistently and believe my faith can move mountains, even if it is only the size of a mustard seed.

> *"He replied, 'Because you have so little faith. Truly I tell you, if you have faith as small as a mustard seed, you can say to this mountain, "Move from here to there," and it will move. Nothing will be impossible for you'" (Matthew 17:20).*

In God's word that's all He asks of us — to have faith at least the size of a mustard seed. I am not perfect. I waver on occasion when the big storms come but can quickly ground myself in prayer and faith in the one who has my destiny in His hands.

I am determined.

Maybe this is a characteristic born from my abuse but give me a challenge and I am like a dog with a bone. I will not give up. I will work my fingers to the bone and come up with plan A, B, C, and D to make it work. Others have often commented that I have the gift of thinking outside the box to solve a problem or address a challenge. I am a real estate broker outside of my ministry, and that trait has served me well in getting deals to the closing table. Rarely do I accept defeat, and when I do, it's not easy.

I have an abundance of compassion.

I feel other people's pain, both emotional and physical, and have a great deal of compassion. Sometimes people just need to talk and so I listen, give them a hug, and they feel a sense of peace. I know that is the Holy Spirit working through me, giving them that comfort. When I pray over them, God intervenes and gives them relief from their pain. I desire to be the hands and feet of Jesus and allow Him to use me as a vessel.

A. W. Tozer wrote in *The Pursuit of God*, "God breathed on clay, and it became a man; He breathes on men, and they become clay." I deeply desire to become clay in the hands of God to be molded into the person He wants me to be, stepping out of my comfort zone to provide hope and healing to a hurting world.

I am courageous.

I have been homeless. I have jumped off of a fifty-foot telephone pole. I have walked on burning coals. I have spoken before large audiences. I have been scuba diving sixty feet below the surface. I whitewater-rafted a class-five rapid and flown in a helicopter to an erupting volcano. I have snow-skied a black diamond run. I have ziplined across the jungle and have taken risks that would make others shiver.

I survived and would do it all again. I am grateful that I live in faith and not fear, and I will embrace the next challenge around the corner with courage.

I am an eternal optimist.

The glass is always half full. I make lemonade

from my life's lemons. I know all things work together for good. If at first I don't succeed, I try, try again. All corny sayings, I know, but I do believe good overcomes evil and that God is in control and things work out the way they are supposed to.

I am adventuresome.

I love a good adventure, to travel to new places, experience new things, and meet new people. It doesn't matter if it's a new restaurant or a new country—it's great fun. I've been blessed to have experienced many adventures in my life.

The most exciting was taking my first whitewater-rafting trip at the height of my healing journey. Not knowing anything about whitewater rafting when I booked my trip, I signed up for a trip with class-five rapids. That would not have been so bad, but I couldn't even swim at the time. It was a great adventure and one that God worked miraculously through, which I journal in my book, *From Sorrows to Sapphires*. I pray I never lose my sense of adventure and am excited for the next adventure God has in store for my life.

I am honest.

I am an honest person, a person of integrity. I value my word and my reputation. I want to be the person others can depend on to always keep my word.

What do you love about you? You may have had your self-confidence and your self-respect damaged by your abuser, but you can recover and recapture all that was lost. Restoring your confidence will help you become all that God has created you to be.

> *"I will restore to you the years that the locust has eaten" (Joel 22:23).*

Before my healing, when I walked into a room, I would second-guess myself, fearing how others would respond to me. I now walk in a room with the confidence that I am accepted and I am loved.

In your quest to love you, I encourage you to write down the things you love about yourself so you can also truly value how very special you are to God and to others.

And if you stumble, know that today is a new day and is much too precious with its hopes and invitations to waste a moment on the failures of yesterday. When you change your relationship with failure and rejection, you change your life. Instead of beating yourself up, instead of spiraling in those moments of failure, reach around and pat yourself on the back, because you are one of the few victorious ones who was brave enough to have the courage to try.

Failure is one step closer to success. Rejection and failure are the best teachers. Failure is the path from underestimated to unstoppable. The meaning you attach to failure can empower you, not defeat you. Release the fear of failure, turn down the volume of self-doubt, and turn up the volume of self-belief. Today is the first day of the rest of your life.

> *"The steadfast love of the Lord never ceases; his mercies never come to an end; they are new every morning; great is your faithfulness. 'The Lord is my portion,' says my soul, 'therefore I will hope in him'"* (Lamentations 3:22–24).

The love within empowers us to love intentionally and create the life we desire.

CHAPTER 9

Love Gives

*"Give **generously** to them and do so without a grudging heart; then because of this the LORD your God will bless you in all your work and in everything you put your hand to" (Deuteronomy 15:10).*

Jesus prophesied that Peter would deny him three times before the rooster crowed. It came to pass that on the night of Jesus's crucifixion, Peter, in his flesh and in his fear denied, knowing Jesus three times. Peter was heartbroken and wept over his weakness. During one of Jesus's post-resurrection appearances, Jesus was with Peter. The conversation with Peter showed great

145

compassion and tenderness. Jesus filled his nets with fish and had hot coals ready to cook breakfast for his disciples. It taught us the most important reflection of love for Jesus.

> *"When they had finished eating, Jesus said to Simon Peter, 'Simon son of John, do you love me more than these?' 'Yes, Lord,' he said, 'you know that I love you.' Jesus said, 'Feed my lambs.'*
>
> *"Again Jesus said, 'Simon son of John, do you love me?' He answered, 'Yes, Lord, you know that I love you.' Jesus said, 'Take care of my sheep.'*
>
> *"The third time he said to him, 'Simon son of John, do you love me?' Peter was hurt because Jesus asked him the third time, 'Do you love me?' He said, 'Lord, you know all things; you know that I love you.' Jesus said, 'Feed my sheep'"* (John 21:15–17).

"Feed my sheep, feed my lambs . . ." Jesus describes His children as sheep, lambs, throughout scriptures. By describing His people as lambs, He is emphasizing their nature as immature and vulnerable and in need of guidance and care. Jesus was instructing Peter to not only care for but pastor and provide spiritual truth from the youngest of the lambs to the full-grown sheep. His calling was to nourish and care for the souls of God's children and to bring them into spiritual maturity.

Whether we are lambs or full-grown sheep, baby Christians or mature Christians, we demonstrate our love for Jesus by sharing truth and the love of Christ Jesus. This love continues to give exponentially in healing lives, restoring families, and fighting evil, in and through us.

> *"Believe me when I say that I am in the Father and the Father is in me; or at least believe on the evidence of the works themselves. Very truly I tell you, whoever believes in me will do the works I have been doing, and they will do even greater things than these, because I am going to the Father. And I will do whatever you ask in my name, so that the Father may be glorified in the Son" (John 13:11–13).*

There were those who took this literally, who cared for me, who mentored me, who taught me, who fed me when I was an infant Christian. I would not be the Godly woman I am today without them being obedient to the words of Jesus, "Feed my sheep." The love they poured into me helped me to truly love myself unconditionally, like God loves me.

Through their love, I have received and now walk in the fruits of the spirit. I believe God listed them in order and the first three, love, joy and peace promote the last six. As you fill yourself with the fruits of the spirit, they will overflow in your life and the lives you touch.

> *"But the fruit of the Spirit is love, joy, peace, forbearance, kindness, goodness, faithfulness, gentleness and self-control. Against such things there is no law"* *(Galatians 5:22–23).*

I was driving in bumper-to-bumper traffic up I-575 North and slightly hit my brake. Suddenly, I was rear-ended. There was nothing I could do, no way to avoid this accident. You can't drive down the road while only looking in the rearview mirror. You have to look ahead.

But sometimes you may get rear-ended with waves of pain from your past. Repressed memories creep in and can be mentally challenging, but this is normal. What we need to focus on is how we respond to these jolts and process them in the healthiest way possible. If you have a plan in place, you can easily take the steps that lead to recovery and healing versus spiraling out of control emotionally. You know the steps you take if you are rear-ended — pull over to the side of the road, check your damage, call the police, take photos, etc. When you are rear-ended with emotional pain, make a plan for the actions you need to take. These actions can include the following:

- Acknowledge you need help.
- Share with a confidant.
- Spend more time with God, in His word and in prayer.
- Make a counseling appointment.
- Indulge in more self-care.
- Be honest about your feelings.

It's important to execute a plan. I see my counselor from time to time as needed. If I feel myself spinning out of control, I seek counseling to help me sort through the chaos and regain my peace.

My weakness is when fear creeps into my life. Fear can be paralyzing. I don't like to feel afraid. I spent so many years terrified of my abuser. He was so cruel; I never knew what horrible rant was coming next.

We need to recognize when we need help, either by helping ourselves or asking for help.

That is part of loving me and taking care of me. Yes, you can say "no," take the day off, go away for a couple nights from family and friends. Loving you is loving spending time with yourself.

One of my precious friends, Annette, taught me so much about how she loves herself. She was always quick to indulge in self-care. Always laughing, smiling, bringing joy. She was a flight attendant, and she loved to treat herself to exotic trips and spa treatments and enjoyed having lunch or dinner by herself. She took great care of herself, physically and emotionally, and she loved who she was in her own skin. All that was so foreign to me because I struggled to spend time alone. She taught me to lay down the guilt around self-care and embrace yourself.

I started slowly and now I love my time alone. It's not a lot of time, a trip here and there, and my husband travels from time to time for business. I absolutely love those times, when I get to do exactly what I want to do. I am so glad Annette lived her best life because God took her home early, as she passed away at fifty-three years old of colon cancer.

Annette was the first person to read my memoir, *From Sorrows to Sapphires*. We were on one of our trips, and we always rented out a two-bedroom suite with a huge deck. We sat on that deck all night as I watched her turn page by page, eating chocolate. Finally, she said, "Angie, this is so good, it has to be published." And every few pages she would repeat it. That was all the confidence I needed and in 2014 I released *From Sorrows to Sapphires*, which chronicles a life-changing weekend of my life when I took a trip by myself down the Oconee River.

A getaway may be just what the doctor ordered for you. Or if that's not possible, indulge in some stay-cation self-care. Maybe book a massage, take a long bath, take a walk, go to an art gallery or antique shop, find a park, dance in the rain. Do whatever makes YOU happy.

When you are on a flight, they always instruct you to put the oxygen mask on yourself first before helping others. Indulge in those small things that help you feel better.

Yesterday is gone, tomorrow is a surprise, and today is the present, a present—the most precious gift you have: time, this very moment. I look back on my life and realize I spent too much time wallowing in the wounding and acting out in unhealthy ways to cope with the pain. If I hit it head on, do all the things I know are the healthiest choices, and keep considering healthy healing options, I will be at peace again. Perfect peace is a struggle for most that have suffered abuse.

I pray this book will be read through the generations and will be a great resource to those who are suffering with the residual pain of abuse. I pray others will gain the strength to stand with me. There are many wonderful warriors and organizations fighting this battle, but not nearly enough for the amount of people who have been victimized. That's why my daily prayer is that survivors heal and rise up. Rise up! My voice, Angela's Voice, is dedicated to breaking the silence of child sexual abuse and provide helpful resources. I desire to be a voice for a silent nation to help them speak.

As an overcomer of abuse, you have so much to give and so much to share, and we can all learn from your journey. There is a movement to advocate for survivors. The following is a short list of organizations you can get involved with in your community to help spread the word and promote great work in the battle of abuse.

April: Child Abuse Awareness Month
https://www.childwelfare.gov/topics/preventing/preventionmonth/

April 30: White Out Child Sexual Abuse Day
angelasvoice.com/events

May: Mental Health Awareness Month
https://www.nami.org/Get-
Involved/Awareness-Events/Mental-Health-
Awareness-Month

October: Domestic Violence Awareness Month
https://www.thehotline.org/stakeholders/d
omestic-violence-awareness-month/

Non-profit organizations always need you to support their cause. Volunteering is a wonderful way to give back and meet people who share your passions to give. You have gifts and talents that are so incredibly valuable to the cause. Love gives and gives.

I love myself when I have the courage to say "yes" to stepping out of my comfort zone to give of myself, my gifts, my talents. If you have been reserved in giving of your time, I encourage you to step out and step up. My experience has been that as I bless others, I am incredibly blessed. Opening your hands and heart to give of your time, talents, and resources is a rewarding experience.

CHAPTER 10

Loves Wins

"May God give you heaven's dew and earth's richness—an abundance of grain and new wine" (Genesis 27:28).

God wants to bless us, overwhelmingly bless us, and give us the desires of our heart with an avalanche of abundance. The greatest of those blessings is to live in peace, with joy. I give God all the praise, honor, and glory for my healing. God is honored when we give Him the glory for our victories.

I am so grateful for my trials and my triumphs for both have made me the person I am today—a person I love, a person I respect, and a person still growing. A person I must consistently extend grace for my failures, for my doubt, for my fear, yet celebrate my successes. Fighting fear with faith is knowing that, in the valleys and on the mountaintops of life, God is with me and has a perfect plan for my life.

> *"God's voice thunders in marvelous ways; he does great things beyond our understanding. He says to the snow, 'Fall on the earth,' and to the rain shower, 'Be a mighty downpour'"* (Job 37:5–6).

Love wins when we love as God loves.

> *"The Lord appeared to us in the past, saying: 'I have loved you with an everlasting love; I have drawn you with unfailing kindness'"* (Jeremiah 31:3).

If no one has ever told you this, please hear me: I am so very sorry that you experienced abuse. I am sorry for the pain and turmoil this has caused in your life. I want to stand in the gap for your abuser and ask for your forgiveness. You may never hear that from your abuser, but I pray that brings you some comfort and that you can release them. You are not in this moment in time by accident. God has a plan and purpose for you and a plan and purpose for me. God will use everything in our lives for His glory.

> *"You intended to harm me, but God intended it for good to accomplish what is now being done, the saving of many lives"* *(Genesis 50:20).*

These are Joseph's words to his brothers amid their abuse. Your testimony, your trials are fuel for healing for both you and those you share your journey with. I pray that the scripture I sprinkled throughout these pages will give you a hunger to read the greatest love story in the world—the Bible, the living, life-giving instruction manual of life, Alfa and Omega, the infinite word of God.

God reminds us that every word He speaks does not come back void. God breathed His word and God's DNA is in His word.

> *"So is my word that goes out from my mouth; it will not return to me empty, but will accomplish what I desire and achieve the purpose for which I sent it. 12 You will go out in joy and be led forth in peace; the mountains and hills will burst into song before you, and all the trees of the field will clap their hands"* *(Isaiah 55:11–12).*

My favorite words are, "You will go out in joy and be led forth in peace." That is my prayer for me and for you. There is no better time to believe again than today. Loving is a gift, and love always wins. God's definition of love is powerful in teaching us how to love. Many call 1 Corinthians the "love chapter."

> *"If I speak in the tongues of men or of angels, but do not have love, I am only a resounding gong or a clanging cymbal. If I have the gift of prophecy and can fathom all mysteries and all knowledge, and if I have a faith that can move mountains, but do not have love, I am nothing. If I give all I possess to the poor and give over my body to hardship that I may boast, but do not have love, I gain nothing.*
>
> *"Love is patient, love is kind. It does not envy, it does not boast, it is not proud. It does not dishonor others, it is not self-seeking, it is not easily angered, it keeps no record of wrongs. Love does not delight in evil but rejoices with the truth. It always protects, always trusts, always hopes, always perseveres.*
>
> *"Love never fails. But where there are prophecies, they will cease; where there are*

tongues, they will be stilled; where there is knowledge, it will pass away. For we know in part and we prophesy in part, but when completeness comes, what is in part disappears. When I was a child, I talked like a child, I thought like a child, I reasoned like a child. When I became a man, I put the ways of childhood behind me. For now we see only a reflection as in a mirror; then we shall see face to face. Now I know in part; then I shall know fully, even as I am fully known.

"And now these three remain: faith, hope and love. But the greatest of these is love" (1 Corinthians 13).

Finally, I leave you with what loving me means:

- *Loving the person God created me to be with no apologies.*
- *Living Jesus's word, way, and walk.*
- *Loving my neighbor as myself.*
- *Protecting me and my peace*
- *Accepting me with all my faults and flaws.*
- *Celebrating me with all my value and success.*
- *Releasing me from shame and bondage.*
- *Self-care without guilt.*
- *Forgiving me when I fail.*
- *Forgiving others when they fail me.*

- *Asking for help without shame.*
- *Making healthy choices to promote a healthy lifestyle.*
- *Courage to chase my dreams.*
- *Letting go of the fear of failure.*
- *Pursuing healing for a lifetime.*
- *Valuing life — past, present, and future.*
- *Breaking every curse spoken over me.*
- *Living life to the fullest and pursuing happiness.*
- *Generously giving of my treasures, time, and talents.*
- *Embracing that I am a beautiful soul with a big heart.*

Please embrace, in your core, that you are important, deserving, loving, intelligent, worthy, compassionate, beautiful, creative, inspiring, brave, true, strong, and able. That is who God created you to be.

I pray that, by reading *Loving Me: After Abuse*, you have begun to embrace your healing journey and make peace with your past. I pray that you will take a deep breath and know that you are not alone in your struggles. I pray my words, my encouragement, my experiences, and my revelations will strengthen you in a way that helps you truly heal and love yourself. I hope you have found a friend in me and that one day we shall meet, and I hope to hear you say, "I'm loving me after abuse."

Loving me means facing trauma with the courage to accept that it changed you, but only for the better, as you have an inner strength that is unshakable. You also have a love that can never be taken away from you, being secure in God's unconditional love without dependence on anyone else. This is the true gift of love—to always know you are loved no matter the circumstances.

God's mercies are new every morning and never change. He is the same yesterday, today, tomorrow, and eternal. There is an expiration date on your suffering, and I pray that day is today. The old story may be that it robbed you, it weakened you, but today you can write a new story, one of courage and strength. This permanent shift can bring you out of the storm into the sun. Hard times are not forever; life is always changing. You are worthy of your hopes and dreams.

The beauty of being the author of your own story is that the next chapter is up to you to write! The best is yet to come.

Love wins.

RESOURCES

Angela's VOICE
angelasvoice.com

Counseling Support
www.betterhelp.com

American Association of Christian Counselors
http://www.aacc.net/resources/find-a-counselor

American Addiction Centers
Projectknow.org

Celebrate Recovery
celebraterecovery.com

Suicide Hotline:
Call 988
988lifeline.org

Child Abuse

All States' Reporting:

Child Welfare (1-800-394-3366)

1-800-FYI-3366

childwelfare.gov

English and Spanish available

Childhelp

childhelp.org

1.800.422.4453

Text 847411, code: ChildHelp

Child Sexual Abuse Stop It Now

stopitnow.org.

1.888.773.8368

National Child's Advocacy Center

nationalcac.org

National Center for Missing & Exploited Children

missingkids.org

1.800. THE-LOST (1.800.843.5678)

English and Spanish available

Domestic Violence
National Domestic Violence Organizations
http://www.nationalcenterdvtraumamh.org/re
sources/national-domestic-violence-
organizations/

National Domestic Violence Hotline
1-800-799SAFE (1-800-799-7233)
English and Spanish available

Abuse Victim Hotline *(free legal advice and counsel)*
1-877-448-8678

Human Trafficking

Polaris
polarisproject.org

National Human Trafficking Hotline
1-888-373-7888

Recommended Child Abuse Prevention Programs:

Internet Safety 101
internetsafety101.org

The two primary internet dangers for children today are their free and easy access to all types of pornography, and sexual predators' easy and anonymous access to children. In this workshop, you learn valuable information, techniques, and skills to help you maintain a safe, entertaining, and informative environment.

Darkness to Light
d2l.org

Stewards of Children's Seven Steps to Prevent Child Sexual Abuse

This workshop is designed to educate adults about the risks of child sexual abuse and to establish a plan of protection for each child. It seeks to remove the responsibility to tell from the child and places it on informed adults who accept the responsibility to be alert, watchful, and prevention/protection-oriented.

ACKNOWLEDGMENTS

With a heart full of gratitude and admiration, I want to acknowledge all those who played a critical role in the publishing of *Loving Me: After Abuse*.

Thank you to my husband, Phil, for being the wind beneath my wings, a constant source of encouragement and love. I thank my children, Ashley and Jacob, who inspire me with their courage and determination to run into the fire of life.

To my amazing publishing team at BookLogix for your incredible commitment, relentless encouragement, and hard work to bring *Loving Me: After Abuse* to the world. I am eternally grateful.

For the most talented and creative artist I have ever met, Shan Wallace, thank you for a beautiful cover that communicates the beauty of freedom when the love for yourself is restored.

For the friends I entrusted to read the first draft of this manuscript—Deborah Griggs,

Lauren Gaines, Pastor Craig Mosgrove, and Theresa Harvard Johnson — I thank you from the bottom of my heart for giving me the confidence to take the next step, encouraging me that the book will bring healing to those suffering. I, too, thank each of you for your endless prayers and Godly wisdom. Pastor Craig Mosgrove, thank you for your Godly counsel, being such a compassionate, caring pastor, and for giving me the courage to pick up the mantle.

ABOUT ANGELA'S VOICE

Angela's Voice is dedicated to developing, distributing, and endorsing valuable resources in the awareness, prevention, and healing of child sexual abuse. The materials, though specific for survivors of child sexual abuse, also benefit any abuse survivor and help protect children by teaching them how to defend themselves from abusive behavior. Founder Angela Williams, MFP, is a survivor-turned-advocate who shares a powerful message of triumph over tragedy by sharing her vulnerable and candid voice about her abuse trauma, her pain, her struggles, and her journey to healing in hopes that it may help other survivors expedite their healing journey.

Angela Williams has devoted years to providing awareness, prevention, and healing programs through her advocacy work. Williams has captivated audiences with her powerful message of triumph over tragedy as a victim of childhood physical and sexual abuse. At age seventeen, she attempted suicide, and that day was the end of her torment and the beginning of a journey to healing. She is a crusader for change and dedicates her life to eradicate child sexual abuse. She holds a master's in forensic psychology with a concentration in child abuse. Williams is a powerful messenger, appearing in national and international news and documentaries. She has been successful in state legislative reform and national policy work and served on the Policy Committee of the National Coalition to Prevent Child Sexual Abuse and Exploitation. She has received numerous accolades and awards for her work, including her collection of books that have valuable lessons for survivors of all ages.

OTHER BOOKS BY
ANGELA WILLIAMS

Loving Me: After Abuse
From Sorrows to Sapphires, Angela Williams's
Memoir

Interactive Workbooks — Adults

Healing
Pathway to Healing, Guide to Healing
True Intimacy
Shattering the Shame
Unveiling Child Sexual Abuse

Prevention
Tough Talk to Tender Hearts
The Grooming Mystery
Single Parenting Solutions
Courage to Speak

Children's Books (Ages 5–10)
Gracie Finds Her Voice
Grant Gets His Shield
Gracie and Grant's Big Win
Gracie and Grant's Big Win Coloring Book
Find Your Voice Curriculum Book

Please follow Angela Williams on social media
and contact angelasvoice.com to book a speaking
event or interview.